D1526831

# MARTIN OPPENHEIMER

# THE STATE IN MODERN SOCIETY

## Humanity Books

an imprint of Prometheus Books
59 John Glenn Drive, Amherst, New York 14228-2197

Published 2000 by Humanity Books, an imprint of Prometheus Books

04 03 02 01 00    5 4 3 2 1

Library of Congress Cataloging-in-Publication Data

Oppenheimer, Martin.
    The state in modern society / Martin Oppenheimer.
      p.   cm.
    Includes bibliographical references and index.
    ISBN 1–57392–822–4 (cloth : alk. paper)
    1. State, The.  2. World politics—20th century.  I. Title.
JC11 .O64 2000
320.1—dc21                                       99–087115
                                                CIP

Printed in the United States of America on acid-free paper

# CONTENTS

# PREFACE

The purpose of this book is to present a general framework through which we can better understand the different forms of the state, or to use the more popular expression, "government," in the twentieth century.[1] Most conventional treatments emphasize the actual structure and functioning of the institutions of the state, differentiating between, say, a presidential and a parliamentary model, or diagramming the policy-making route between a congress and an executive, or contrasting among different kinds of dictatorships based on their ideology (communism versus fascism, for instance), or the relationship of various forces to the state (whether the party, the military, or the governmental administrators have more power). The present work departs from those models and focuses on that unpleasant and somewhat unfashionable dimension called "class." Readers who are familiar with similar works in the past will recognize that this focus is based on Marxian theory.

Most work that has focused on the relationship between class and state has concentrated on single examples and single countries. There are a great many such analyses, beginning with the writings of Marx and Engels.[2] These continue to be models for many writers with a left perspective, and will be referenced throughout this book as appropriate. Others in this tradition have focused on particular dimensions of state policy (for instance, the treatment of the poor, the "criminal justice" system, organized labor, civil and minority rights, the "national question," gender issues, social movements more generally, power structures, and of course imperialism and war). These authors, too, will be referred to when appropriate. This book is one of the very few that tries to deal in a comparative way with an entire set of types of states in modern times in the context of class relationships.[3]

In developing a framework that will help understand these different types of state, I have made a lot of pretty broad generalizations. Oversimplification is always a danger in a work of this kind, but it is a risk that must be taken, albeit with care, because the overriding desire here is to make the ideas involved in the political sociology of the state accessible to a wider audience that is rightfully disdainful of nit-picking scholasticism written solely for academic insiders and for the sake of professional advancement. Almost needless to say, in trying to present a general framework of this kind, arguments can be raised about many specifics. I welcome such criticisms so long as the critics understand and sympathize with the purpose of this book. Friendly criticism from establishment academics whose work is rooted in status quo social science is not likely, since their basic assumptions about how society works are so distantly removed from those in this book that we speak virtually different languages.

Despite what I have said about making the work accessible, there is extensive footnoting. The purpose of the footnotes is primarily to provide guidance to readers who want to follow up on their own with readings on a given point, rather than, as is often the case, to give the appearance of credibility and academic respectability. In any case, direct quotations always require attribution.

Readers will note that there is little material in this book dealing with the nations of the African continent. The slave trade and its historical consequences, which continue to this day, constitutes a vast

and complex subject. Like too many U.S. social scientists, unfortunately, I have little expertise in this area. South Africa is a better-
known case, but as an extreme instance of a "racial state" it presents
complexities that do not fit readily into the framework of this book.
Intensive further research would be needed in order to attain some
clarity. All African states have at some time been colonies, and their
artificial boundaries, drawn by their European conquerors, have created a series of national minority problems that will be touched on
in chapter 7. Almost all have evolved into dictatorships that differ
mainly in their degree of corruption, repressiveness, and the emiseration of their populations, the heritage of colonial exploitation;
this form of dictatorship will be examined later.

Another topic that readers will find all too thinly described and
analyzed is Yugoslavia. The collapse of Tito's "Communist" regime
triggered a series of wars and ethnic "cleansings" within and
between several of the former constituent states of the Yugoslav federation. The most recent of these human catastrophes has been the
1999 explusion of the Albanian Kosovar population of Yugoslavia by
the Serbian state, and the resultant war on Serbia by the North
Atlantic Treaty Organization, led by the United States. Although
these events are touched on in chapter 7, and an attempt is made
there to integrate them into the framework of this book, this effort is
necessarily sketchy, not to mention risky, and it may even be out-
dated by the time this book appears.

I am greatly indebted to a number of people for providing
advice, support, inspiration, criticism, and above all discussions and
writings from which I have learned tremendously. A number of colleagues and former graduate students at Rutgers University were
invaluable especially in the shaping of chapter 2 on the "National
Security State": Jane C. Canning, James D. Cockcroft, and Dale L.
Johnson. Chapter 4 on power structures was greatly influenced by
the work (and personal encouragement) of G. William Domhoff.
Chapter 5 goes back to a year as a graduate student at Columbia
University, where I had a course with Seymour Martin Lipset, the

readings for which helped to shape my thinking considerably and motivated me to explore the Nazi movement further. I acquired my basic theoretical understanding of Stalinism (as distinct from the facts, which I already knew about), from the circle of people associated with Max Shachtman's organization, the Independent Socialist League, and its informal youth group, the Young Socialist League, from some "libertarian socialists," and from a handful of democratic socialists in or around the Socialist Party in the 1950s. I particularly want to mention Henry Radetsky; the late Leo Kormis; Edmund I. Gordon (wherever he is), who gave me access to archival material that included back issues of *Politics* magazine, the *Young Socialist Review*, and other obscure magazines on the left; and of course the late Max Shachtman himself. My appreciation of Rosa Luxemburg initially came from discussions with Bogdan Denitch, then a machinist and later a faculty member at the City University of New York, and more recently from reading the work of Stephen Eric Bronner of Rutgers University. My most sympathetic supporter in this project has been my wife, partner, and comrade, Hannah Fink.

The writing of this book was greatly facilitated by a Faculty Academic Study Program Leave, and a Competitive Fellowship Leave, from Rutgers University, and by a Fulbright Award in 1998.

I am also grateful to a handful of friends over the years who from time to time have complained that there was no easy-to-understand book that would explain what Marxists or leftists had to say about how society works. There are a few, of course. Hopefully this book will augment that list.

## NOTES

1. "Government" and "state" are not synonymous. See chapter 1 for more on this.

2. For example, Frederick Engels, *The Peasant War in Germany* (Moscow: Foreign Languages Publishing House, 1956 ed.), written in 1850;

Karl Marx, *The Class Struggles in France* and *The Eighteenth Brumaire of Louis Bonaparte* (London: Lawrence and Wishart, Ltd., 1950 ed.), written in 1850 and 1851 respectively, and of course *Capital* itself. Another classic Marxist study is Leon Trotsky, *The History of the Russian Revolution* (Ann Arbor, Mich.: University of Michigan Press, n.d.; Simon and Schuster, 1932).

3. For a somewhat different kind of comparative approach, see Berch Berberoglu, *Political Sociology* (Dix Hills, N.Y.: General Hall, Inc., 1990). Berberoglu's chapter 7 on "The Socialist State," however, differs from chapter 6 in the present volume not only in its comparative style. His description of the Soviet Union and the People's Republic of China as having been engaged in "socialist construction" is little more than an apology for the horrors inflicted on the peoples of both countries by their respective dictatorships, one that is possible only by ignoring an ocean of facts.

# 1
# INTRODUCTION: STATE, CLASS, AND REVOLUTION

*Since the power of the ruling class is always concentrated in the organization of the state, the oppressed class must aim directly at the mechanism of the state. Every class struggle is thus a* political struggle, *which in its objectives aims at the abolition of the existing order and at the establishment of a new social system.*

—Leon Trotsky[1]

If the history of all hitherto existing literate society is the history of class struggle, it follows that the history of all states is that of revolution, the most important outcome of class struggle. That is, all states are the embodiment of struggles between classes that have in the past culminated in some form of revolution, and in turn every revolution creates a new state in the image, no matter how imperfect, of whatever class or classes are triumphant. If no class is strong enough to triumph, a state that acts as a temporary bridge to whatever class becomes ripe for power at a later point is created (Bonapartism). If the class that has made a revolution, and created a state in its own interest, is too weak to dominate its state, another class may develop to usurp power, and alter the state to meet its requirements (Stalinism in its various forms). If an established ruling class is no longer capable of managing a stable state, it may call into existence a dictatorship to act on its behalf (fascism).

No state has come into existence representing, at its birth, an unequivocal, totally successful revolution representing the complete triumph of a revolutionary class. All revolutions have been partial at best. As often as not, revolutions fail, and the victory of counterrevolution marks the return, at least briefly, to the previous order, and the state that embodies that order.

What is revolution, and what is the state? Revolution is a sudden, dramatic overturn of the existing state apparatus *that represents an overthrow of the dominant social class and its displacement.* The assumption is that all states represent, in their form, personnel, and policy, sometimes to a greater degree, sometimes to a lesser, and no matter how imperfectly, the ruling class or (sometimes in combination) classes of their time. The definition of a state, therefore, is complex: in common, everyday language we sometimes refer to governments, or "the public sector," which is appropriate enough when referring to the specific *form* of a state (that is, its bureaucratic institutions), or to its *fiscal* nature (to distinguish its institutions and personnel from the private sector), but this is overly static. The term *state* has a more dynamic implication: it is joined to the concept of power, and to the assumption that in class societies there will be a set of institutions that will exert power in the interest of ruling elites and against those seeking to alter the existing order. That set of institutions is called the state. The power that the state is able to exercise is ultimately that of coercion, of military force, of violence. The state is therefore frequently defined as the holder of a monopoly of the "legitimate," that is, ordained or legislated, use of violence.

States exist, therefore, whenever there is a class structure in which classes (plural) contend for domination. If there are no classes (as in many preliterate societies), that is, if all people share the same relationship to nature, and property is held more or less in common, so that there is in a sense only one class, there is no need for a state because there is no need for one group to protect its interests from another.

In class societies, at any given moment one class either dominates (however shakily), and writes the rules of how "its" state functions, or no class is capable of dominating, in which case the state is, at least temporarily, independent or autonomous, floating, in a sense, above classes. But the normal condition is one in which "society has become entangled in an insoluble contradiction with itself, that it is cleft into irreconcilable antagonisms," as Engels phrased it, so that a state is necessary to "moderate" the conflict.[2] But it does not moderate it in order to conciliate the classes: instead it "moderates" by way of maintaining "order" for the purpose of enabling one class to oppress the others.

When social, economic, and political forces develop that make a ruling class, and its state, incapable of carrying out its common task (which is at minimum to assure the basic stability that is required for the survival of that ruling class), those forces congeal to generate political movements and contest for state power. But since the existing state apparatus is functional only for the rule of the old regime, it is almost inevitable that a political movement representing a different class will have to replace that state with another that is appropriate to its own agenda, following a successful revolution.

A coup d'etat, or its parliamentary parallel, a change in the political party that runs the government, the state bureaucracy, is therefore not a revolution, since such a change does not represent a fundamental structural shift in the nature of the dominant class. The same class continues to rule, although the particular *fraction*, or segment of the ruling class that dominates the state may change. But even civil wars, like the bloody one in the United States in 1861 or the shorter ones in Chile in 1851, 1859, and 1891, do not necessarily herald a fundamental change in the nature of the ruling class, although they do represent a shift of power within or among ruling-class fractions.[3]

By this definition, the Nazi "revolution," as it is called by many, was no revolution at all. Even though mass based, even though it fundamentally changed the structure of the state, the old ruling class of industrialists and landlords continued to dominate the economic system, albeit in a restricted way. To an extent, the old ruling class lost control of the state, which behaved, as many scholars see it, independently in the sense that although the basic assumptions of capitalism were not challenged, at least some of the state's major policy decisions were made even though they damaged some segments of capital.

Conflicts such as civil wars and coups, even the displacement of parliamentary democracy with fascist dictatorship, frequently represent a shift in the configuration of power among the different fractions of the ruling class, for the ruling class is never completely homogeneous or monolithic. Such internal conflicts result not just in changes in personnel, or in comparatively minor policies, but may also reflect the rise and fall of different parts of a dominant class. The triumph of the North in the U.S. Civil War marked the hegemony of industrial capital over all other fractions of capital, most especially the Southern, slave-holding plantations. It represented the victory of the exploiters of wage slavery over exploiters of chattel slavery. Chile's series of civil wars, by contrast, constituted successive defeats of the modern bourgeoisie at the hands of the landed bourgeoisie. The 1891 conflict also involved foreign capital. In the United States, the recent victories of the Republican Party represent the relative political weakening of fractions of capital historically committed to minimal reformism, in the context of the globalization of capital (of which more later), even though the overall domination of Eastern industrial and finance capital (in the form of multinational corporations) remains fundamentally unshaken: both parties support "globalization," with minor differences in the rules under which it is to take place.

History has amply demonstrated the proposition that the overthrow of a government, and the demise of the ruling class for which it is the general agent, does not necessarily mean that another class is sufficiently strong economically, politically, socially, and ideologically to seize the reins of state power. And even if it is, it may not be strong enough to carry through its class agenda, which is to create a state and a society in its own image, consistent with its own economic imperatives.

Complicating things further is the fact that most "models" of revolution (for instance, the idea that France and Britain represent "classical" bourgeois revolutions) turn out to be quite imperfect. As one historian has remarked, although England was the first capitalist country, its capitalists were rooted in the aristocratic countryside; and although in France the urban bourgeoisie triumphed, it was mainly composed of professionals, who were not capitalists in the modern sense either.[4] Barrington Moore, one of the most important contributors to the knowledge of revolution, has amply documented the variety of class configurations that can promote what is loosely called "bourgeois revolution," with the key variable being, for him, the varying roles of the landed upper class, and the peasantry.[5]

These complications result in revolutions that are usually incomplete and imperfect, at least initially. Therefore the states that are created in their names are also imperfect, in the sense that they cannot fully represent the class that is responsible for the revolution. It is the unusual state that truly and fully represents, in both its form and its policies, the interests of a coherent, class-conscious, "ripe" ruling class. Even where such a congruence between state and ruling class develops over time, it proves to be relatively short-lived (although some would argue that one hundred years, or even seventy-five, is not so short) because even in the moment of its final triumph, dynamic forces for change are already fully at work to destabilize the new status quo. It then becomes the function of the state to attempt to repress, control, channel, and coopt those forces, both material (technological) and human (movements) if it can.

The key question determining the nature of the state after a revolution is, inevitably: is the new ruling class capable of ruling in its own name? Is it capable of carrying through its own revolution through its own state? To answer this question it is necessary to identify the class that is presumably the revolutionary one.

The overthrow of feudalism (and its partner economic form, landlordism) has been undertaken in different periods and places by a number of different classes under a variety of historical circumstances, some more fortuitous, some less so. In some countries, feudalism and industrial capitalism to some extent developed a partnership and therefore two theoretically incompatible classes were able to coexist, even to merge. As Moore points out, elements of the British landed upper class either joined in the development of modern parliamentary capitalism, or in some cases were swept aside. This alliance, he argues, was successful in creating the modern British state. Where, however, such a mixture contains a relatively weak bourgeois component, and its quasi-parliamentary state confronts a major crisis such as war, a different configuration of revolutionary class forces (including the working class and the peasantry) may develop to overthrow the not-yet-completed bourgeois revolution, as in Russia. In countries where a nascent bourgeoisie confronted a decaying feudalism as its main or sole enemy, as was more the case in France and the United States, a "cleaner" parliamentary state without the accoutrements of feudalism (the continued role of the nobility) was created.

The following "models" (given all the reservations mentioned above) may be helpful in sorting out these differing circumstances:

The American and French cases are often said to be better models of the classical bourgeois revolutions than Britain. The revolutionary class (despite its internal conflicts), aided by the peasantry (which did most of the fighting), carried through revolutions in order to throw off the shackles, as the saying goes, of the restrictions of feudal monarchies in order to create modern nation-states that would carry out the bourgeois agenda of the development of capitalism. In the case of France, moreover, the feudal order was linked to the Roman Catholic Church, and bourgeois rule implied and ultimately required secular rule, as it generally does, in order to overcome theocratic structures that inhibit "rational" capitalist development. In the United States, the bourgeois revolution, secular from the first, was aided and abetted by a local quasi-feudal class, the slaveowner-landlords, many of whom nevertheless were opposed to their English counterparts for economic reasons. We must remember, however, that large segments of the colonist ruling classes sided with the British, and upon their defeat fled the country.

Neither revolution was complete. While the American revolution remained merely uncompleted, the French suffered the victory of counterrevolutionary forces. After the defeat of Napoleon and the creation of the Holy Alliance of the European superpowers Austria, Prussia, and Russia in 1815, it took thirty-three more years for the French finally to oust their last king, Louis-Philippe. Eighteen forty-eight marked a new wave of attempts by bourgeois and working-class elements to extort reforms from their respective rulers, as insurrections swept Europe, triggered by the Paris uprising on February 23. Although the French established a republic, the Second, secured universal manhood suffrage, and banned slavery in their colonies, certainly major reforms on the road to modern society, its bourgeoisie, frightened that its very success would unleash plebeian forces that it could not control, elected the soon-to-be dictator Louis-Napoleon as president later that same year. The French bourgeoisie was not yet ready to rule in its own name.

Even the abolition of slavery was hardly due to the beneficence of France's rulers. Robespierre had emancipated the slaves in French colonies in 1794, but French colonists forced the reintroduction of slavery in 1802. Only in the face of widespread slave revolts in 1848 was slavery finally ended.

The 1848 uprisings in the various states of Germany ended even more equivocally. Frederick William IV of Prussia understood, as George III of England had not, the power of cooptation, and gave permission for indirect elections to state and national parliaments. But by the summer of 1848 most of the European monarchs had had enough of these parliamentary debating societies. Austrian troops suppressed an uprising of Czechs. Then the Austrians defeated the rebellious Italians. In October, Emperor Ferdinand I suppressed the Vienna insurrection. On November 10, King Friedrich William IV's troops reoccupied Berlin, and by the following July all local rebellions throughout the German kingdoms had been put down. Many of the leaders succeeded in fleeing to the United States; one of them, Carl Schurtz, eventually became Secretary of the Interior.

At least part of these setbacks to the German bourgeoisie can be attributed to its comparative isolation from the mass of the population, which was not much interested in the abolition of the monarchy, especially after the Prussian king "gave" Prussia a constitution of sorts. As Bismarck later put it, in Prussia revolutions are made only by kings. It was not until Emperor William II forced Bismarck's retirement in 1890 that the Social Democratic Party, which would soon become Germany's largest parliamentary fraction, was permitted the free air of legality in the new bourgeois German empire. The old monarchy survived even more successfully with a parliament than it had without, until the catastrophe of World War I.

The bourgeois French revolution, while complete from an economic and political standpoint by the time of that war, was probably not fully complete in the important dimension of imposing its culture on the country until after World War II, if then.

In the United States the bourgeois alliance with the slave-owning planters created a contradiction that also prevented the revolution from being carried out fully. A civil war had to take place before capitalism in its modern sense triumphed, and even then, many would say that still another conflict had to take place: the civil rights movement of the 1960s performed the political task that Northern capital had accomplished on the economic front, finally ending the rule of the Southern landed aristocracy.

Other Western countries (and Japan) were even less successful, at least initially, in their bourgeois revolutions. The famous remark of Engels about the German bourgeoisie is to the point: They didn't have the stuff (to rule). Vestiges of feudalism remained (and indeed remain today, at least in symbolic form) in most Western European countries and in Japan, although for practical purposes feudalism was pretty much finished in these countries by the end of the First World War. In almost all of these countries the bourgeoisie, the revolutionary class vis-à-vis feudalism, was too weak to create regimes appropriate to its class interest, yet over time parliamentary states did displace Bonapartism. At the same time, as Moore argues, such revolutions from above culminated, in both Germany and Japan, in one or another type of fascism, albeit short-lived.

When the bourgeoisie of a particular nation is, or becomes, capable of carrying through its revolution and ruling in its own name, the bourgeois state is parliamentary in form. The parliamentary or republican state is the arena in which various fractions of the bourgeoisie (and fractions of other classes that are integrated within the system, such as farmers, the petty bourgeoisie, and even segments of the organized working class) adjudicate their differences and develop a consensus as to social policy. Nevertheless, one fraction generally dominates this "pluralism at the top": an amalgamated union of large industrial and financial corporations, operating through a set of institutions (advisory commissions, philanthropic foundations, universities, cultural institutions including the media, various agencies of the state, and even private clubs and dueling societies!) that it controls directly or via overlapping personnel (see chapter 4). The collapse of this consensus in the face of a major economic crisis, accompanied by a significant growth of potentially revolutionary movements on the Left and extreme "Right" leads to parliamentary disarray and chaos. Given the choice between governmental chaos, the reds, or fascism, the dominant fraction of capital sometimes chooses to dispense with parliament and opts for fascism. One recalls with some dismay the fact that members of the French bourgeoisie (including its military), confronted with an elected reformist Popular Front government led by a moderate socialist, Leon Blum, in the mid-1930s, were quoted as saying, "Better Hitler than Blum." One result of this attitude was the creation of the puppet Vichy regime in the southern part of France after the German military victory early in World War II. Nor was the British aristocracy any less pro-Nazi in the 1930s. Britain's capitulation to Hitler's demands at Munich was therefore not the result of the "weakness" of the democracies, their lack of "moral fiber" as many would have it, but rather due to the class sympathies of some of its "leaders."

In a country like Mexico the Bonapartist model assumes a more graphic form than in France, Germany, or Japan. The Mexican model is one of a succession of failed bourgeois revolutions: the one against the Spanish crown (1812–1820) ended in war-lordism. The one of Benito Juarez (1857) gave way to the corrupt dictatorship of Porfirio Diaz, whose Bismarckian contribution was to sell Mexico out to foreign capital and sugar and other landed barons. In turn, their expropriation of small-scale farmers in the interest of large-scale agribusiness drove villagers (Emiliano Zapata was one) to support revolution. The Madero revolution of 1910, which overthrew Diaz, became a bloody and protracted civil war that ended with a series of Bonapartes (Carranza, Obregon, and subsequent dictators). The rule of the Mexican bourgeoisie was incomplete for many years because the bourgeoisie itself was incomplete. No fraction of capital, much less any other class, was strong enough to create a state in its own image. Hence the Bonapartes. Only by the 1940s was a somewhat more stable development of modern capitalism possible. But even today, with all of the "advantages" of the North American Free Trade Agreement (many of which accrue to foreigners and some sections of the Mexican national bourgeoisie rather than to the bulk of the population), the class rule of the Mexican bourgeoisie is only shakily consolidated by way of corrupt elections and repression.

In other "Third World" countries the development of national bourgeoisies was even more constricted than in Mexico. Colonialism imposed social structures that would in most cases later lead to a distorted, dependent form of development such that independent bourgeoisies on the American, English, or French models could not appear, or if they did appear, would be defeated, hence, the parliamentary state that is appropriate to such a model also appears only as an exception, or only as a "front" for military oligarchies and/or foreign interests. Even in Chile, where a parliamentary structure existed for more than a century (until its overthrow by the Pinochet dictatorship in 1973), it was more often than not the instrument of large landlords; the civil wars that marred its republican history marked the defeats of bourgeois revolutions.

In extreme cases, such as South Korea, foreign occupation precluded local capitalist development for many decades. Bonapartist military dictatorships that succeeded the defeated foreign occupiers (Japan in this case) had first to prepare the soil for local capitalist development (by restricting the role of foreign capital). Only then, and only under rigid state supervision, did native capital gradually come to dominate the society. In still another Bonapartist configuration, the military pretty much became synonymous with local capital (or, conversely, local capital became synonymous with military rule) so that, as in Nicaragua or El Salvador, or in some African countries, Bonapartism functioned not to develop capitalism, but to distort it into a vast, corrupt racket funneling the proceeds of agriculture (sometimes including drugs) into the pockets of a tiny minority that ruled (and in some countries continues to rule) by sheer terror. Protracted revolutionary guerrilla warfare at best, and large-scale banditry and warlordism at worst, inevitably ensued. In the case of Cuba, among others, foreign capital (mainly agribusiness) aligned itself with local military oligarchies, only to be doomed to expropriation (at least for a time) when that oligarchy (installed by foreign capital in the first place) fell to "popular forces," in particular peasant revolutionaries.

Most "Third World" countries, however, fall into neither the South Korean (pure Bonapartism leading to the development of local capitalism) nor the Nicaraguan (corrupt Bonapartism leading to a stunted military-capitalism that would be overthrown by the Sandinistas) models. The model with which we are most familiar (to be dealt with in some detail in the next chapter) is that of "dependent development." In brief, this is a model in which foreign capital distorts the development of a local capitalist class in such a way that its development is largely or entirely subordinate to the needs of capital in the "metropolis" of New York, London, etc. This kind of development assumes that local (native) labor, whether in extractive industries such as agriculture or minerals, or in the assembly of manufactured goods, will remain cheap; hence, it assumes weak labor unions and a strong military to assure social control. Foreign capital, aided by its respective states, attempts to insure that such social control remains in place, if necessary by force, by preventing or suppressing local reform movements. Local bourgeoisies are therefore displaced in those cases where they have economic significance, or prevented (by foreign capital) from ruling in the first place. Only at a later point, as foreign investment flows in and begins to create a modern economic infrastructure, does a local bourgeoisie become significant. But when it does ultimately come to dominate the state, it is within the rigid rules of an international capitalist order that requires the subordination of that bourgeoisie (and its proletariat) to the strictures of the global marketplace, including very importantly the global financial marketplace.

When the bourgeoisie, therefore, is *not yet* capable of ruling in its own name, the consequence is a Bonapartist dictatorship, which, under the best of circumstances, has as its primary function the preparation of bourgeois society and the creation of a republican state. When a national bourgeoisie is *not permitted* to rule because the economy is dominated by foreign capital, the result is a dependent, corrupt dictatorship (or pseudoparliament), the purpose of which is to assure domestic stability and a favorable climate for continued foreign investment. This form may in time be overthrown and displaced by a bourgeois state that is, however, still vulnerable to the global marketplace and its vagaries.

In the twentieth century two other forms of dictatorship arose, with consequences far more horrible than even the worst evils associated with contemporary Third World dictatorships. Following the First World War, the capitalist nations entered a period of acute economic crisis. In some of those nations (with Germany as the extreme case) the crisis was so deep that the bourgeoisie appeared to be *no longer* capable of ruling. In this particular historical circumstance the state was unable to cope with the economic crisis and rapidly lost legitimacy in the eyes of large segments of the population, generating vast movements on the Left threatening the overthrow of capitalism itself. The state appeared incapable of coopting, or suppressing those movements. At the same time alternative movements of a reactionary and ultranationalistic character arose on the "Right." The collapse of the consensus of capitalist pluralism at the top led to the Hitlerian dictatorship, the primary function of which was to rescue bourgeois society by suppressing the Left, but at the price of the abandonment of the republic, and, soon enough, the cost of a devastating war. (More on this form in chapter 5.)

The closing years of World War I saw the Russian monarchic state, representing a corrupt and outmoded feudal order allied with a growing native bourgeoisie (and extensive foreign investment), in deep crisis. The monarchy was swept away in the February 1917 revolution, which can be viewed as an attempt at a classical bourgeois revolution. But the provisional government, the bourgeois state, was also *not yet* capable of solving the basic problems of the society, which in the first instance meant ending the war, and in the second, achieving land reform. Attempts at a classical Bonapartist solution (generals on horseback) collapsed in the face of large-scale revolutionary activity, led by the Bolsheviks. The working class and other popular forces (the peasantry, and dissident elements in the armed forces) were sufficiently powerful to oust the bourgeois government and create a new state structure appropriate to class rule by the proletariat and the peasantry: the Soviet system. However, although strong enough to make a revolution, the working class was also *not yet* strong enough to rule in its own name, particulary following a devastating civil war (against counterrevolutionary forces) in which its leading elements were decimated. In fact, no traditional class in the early years of the Soviet Union was strong enough to impose its rule on the society. Instead, in the absence of a politically organized bourgeoisie (which had been defeated, together with the nobility, in the civil war), and given the weakness of the working class, a new class, that of the bureaucratic managers of the Soviet state, gradually emerged to consolidate its power over the society and turn the Soviet state into its own dictatorship, with consequences (purges, the Gulag, etc.) that became apparent to those with eyes to see by the late 1930s.

There have been several cases in this century in which a revolutionary peasantry has been the main engine for the overthrow of a weak bourgeoisie, often allied to a corrupt and outmoded landlord class (as in China). Here, too, the active revolutionary class was unable to maintain itself in power because, as Marx said long ago, its mode of production isolates peasants from one another so that they are "incapable of enforcing their class interest in their own name," consequently "they must be represented."[6] Marx was referring to classical Bonapartism, in France, but when capitalism is completely destroyed, as in Russia or China, a different form of "representation" arises: the political movement and party that leads the revolution, in short, the Communist or (after some Third World revolutions) the National Independence party comes to rule, and to dominate, and gradually to evolve into a new ruling class.

Therefore, in a society in which the working class is *not yet* or *no longer* capable of ruling in its own name (the peasantry being excluded from such a prospect), the bureaucracy of the party assumes power and, given its monopoly over state-owned capital, assumes the role of a new ruling class, neither a capitalist bourgeoisie, nor a dictatorship of the proletariat, but a dictatorship of the bureaucracy. (See chapter 6.)

In contemporary society, the globalization of capital has put into question the very concept of a "national bourgeoisie." So far, "globalization" has not made national bourgeoisies, and therefore national states, redundant, even though there is a growing international (jet-setting, and not nationally bound) bourgeoisie. The national state, whether of parliamentary, or of oligarchic-military, or of quasi-fascist form, still represents local ruling classes, but it does so more and more by acting as their agents in the international arena, as local ruling classes become global players. The question that this new situation raises is this: will the internationalization of capital allow national states a continuing important role in representing nationally based capitalist classes, or will global capitalism come to dominate national states and turn them into its subordinates? In either case, the accompanying question is: will the internationalization of capital generate its contradiction, an international labor movement that is capable of contesting the agenda of global, "one-world" capital? So far this has not happened. (This issue will be discussed more fully in the Epilogue.)

To summarize: In modern, postfeudal society, if the bourgeoisie is *not yet* strong enough, the outcome is some form of Bonapartist dictatorship. If it is *not allowed* (by foreign capital) to rule, the outcome is a dictatorship that suppresses all domestic classes while acting as a corrupt partner to international capital. If it is *no longer* capable of ruling, the result can be another type of dictatorship, fascism. If it is not yet, or no longer capable of rule but revolutionary movements succeed in preventing, or supplanting dictatorships (including foreign occupation), and in turn those movements are *not yet* or *no longer* capable of ruling in some representative or democratic form, the consequence is a dictatorship of the party that claims to represent the revolution, and the development of that party-state into a "new class." The stability or permanence of that class and its state is subject to the same kinds of stresses that confront all class states, although the form of those conflicts will differ because the configuration of subordinate class forces is different.

This is the formulation that constitutes the framework of the present work. That framework will be elaborated in the next chapter. In that chapter the model of the dependent, "Third World" bourgeois state in its dictatorial or quasi-parliamentary form will be described in greater detail, with some attention, also, to several "exceptions." In chapter 3 the parliamentary bourgeois state of the "advanced" countries, which is theorized to be in a condition of permanent, though not always visible, crisis will be analyzed. This is a less brutal, more enlightened, "friendly" kind of dictatorship even when it is in republican guise. The question mark in the title of the chapter suggests that we need to examine the "fascist" label more carefully when referring to this kind of society.

Chapter 4 will shift the discussion of the bourgeois state somewhat in an examination of its linkages to its corporate masters. The debate about this linkage will be described, and some empirical work will be cited in support of one side, broadly speaking, of the debate. The proposal will be that if the bourgeois state is in fact closely interconnected with one particular fraction of capital (so that its personnel are not only interchangeable but virtually indistinguishable), the "friendly" fascism idea discussed in the previous chapter has at least some validity, even though complete hegemony is precluded by the development of mass movements that must be either repressed or, preferably (in the friendly model) coopted. As President Franklin D. Roosevelt said, "Reform if you would preserve."

This form of state will be carefully distinguished from actual fascism, the subject of chapter 5. Both the social movement that arises in the crisis of "late capitalism" and the form of state that comes to power as the result of a fascist "revolution" will be described and analyzed. The issue of the class nature of the fascist state, or the degree to which it is (still) a capitalist state, versus the degree to which it is autonomous, will be reviewed.

In chapter 6 the class nature of the former Soviet Union, and states of that type such as the People's Republic of China and Cuba, will be examined. The history of the debate as to the class character of the Soviet state will be the subject of one part of the chapter. Some of the reasons for the collapse of the Soviet "empire" will be examined, and an attempt will be made to provide a description of the class nature of the states that have evolved following that collapse.

Finally, in the modern world the issue of the state cannot be adequately addressed without attention to the question of minorities and minority nationalities. That is the subject of chapter 7. A descriptive typology will be integrated with a discussion of the roots of the "minority" or as some would prefer, the "national" question, as well as how state policy toward minorities and subordinate nationalities (including immigration policy) is formed.

In the Epilogue some current questions will be addressed, albeit briefly: In which direction will the various bourgeois-type states go? What does the current backlash against the austerity or Thatcherite model portend? Will the friendlier parliamentary state return to the path of social-democracy, of state intervention, or will it move further toward a privatized corporate dictatorship (sometimes characterized as "neoliberalism")? Will autocratic Third World states be gradually democratized under the influence of the global economy? If economic crisis deepens, will fascism recur? How will modern states cope with the fact of their ethnic, national, etc., heterogeneity? Will bourgeois internationalism in the form of the "global factory" dominate bourgeois nationalism in the form of national chauvinism and xenophobia? Clearly these questions properly deserve a second book, but at least some preliminary thoughts will be attempted.

## NOTES

1. Quoted in Oliver C. Cox, *Caste, Class, and Race* (New York: Modern Reader Paperbacks, 1970), 155.

2. Frederich Engels, *Origins of Family, Private Property, and the State*, in *Karl Marx and Frederick Engels, Selected Works*, vol. 2 (London: Lawrence and Wishart, 1950), 288–89. Quoted in V. I. Lenin, *The State and Revolution*, in *The Essentials of Lenin*, vol. 2 (London: Lawrence and Wishart, 1947), 144. Also in *Lenin, Selected Works* (Moscow: Progress Publishers, 1975), 266, and other sources.

3. Maurice Zeitlin, *The Civil Wars in Chile* (Princeton, N.J.: Princeton University Press, 1984).

4. Claudio J. Katz, review of *The Pristine Culture of Capitalism,* by Ellen Meiskins Wood, *Science & Society* 57, no. 4 (Winter 1993–94): 482.

5. Barrington Moore Jr., *Social Origins of Dictatorship and Democracy* (Boston: Beacon Press, 1966).

6. Karl Marx, *The Eighteenth Brumaire of Louis Bonaparte,* in Karl Marx and Frederick Engels, *Selected Works,* vol. 1 (London: Lawrence & Wishart, 1950), 303.

# 2
# THE NATIONAL
# SECURITY STATE

W e are today witnessing once-powerful societies in the process of losing strength, moving toward crisis. The political or state structures that are characteristic of this new epoch take one of two forms: the openly authoritarian and repressive states of the so-called Third World, and the parliamentary republics of the First World. Yet that is clearly an oversimplification, for not only are there subdivisions within each broad type, but there are also the states of the post-Soviet Second World that do not fit into any neat classification.

The term "national security state" will serve as shorthand for capitalist states of the Third World that are of the authoritarian type. Most of these states promote economic policies of a relatively laissez-faire or "neoliberal" kind, in the interest of their (relatively weak and underdeveloped) national bourgeoisies that are linked to and dependent on international capital. Their authoritarian and repressive character is a symptom of the need to suppress mass discontent and, especially in the current period of global competition, organized labor, so as to continue to keep labor costs cheap. The fact is, however, that brutality and corruption inevitably generate revolutionary activity, including guerrilla warfare, and the economic disruptions and distortions of a country being torn apart by such civil strife are not conducive to a "favorable climate of investment." The consequence is that civilian regimes have increasingly displaced open dictatorships. However, these civilian and ostensibly democratic governments are often just as dictatorial as their uniformed predecessors, as in Peru, or, as in Chile, remain subject to veto (and possible coup) from the military which stands behind these governments and acts as ultimate guarantor of stability.

There is a variant that, while authoritarian, involves a considerable amount of state intervention and is therefore by no means laissez-faire. The model here is South Korea, but Singapore and to a lesser extent Taiwan also share many of the same characteristics. For peculiar and specific historic reasons, these societies have chosen a path to development in which, in order to protect its own bourgeoisie, the state has played an active role in planning the economy and in restricting and controlling foreign investment. The result has been that the populations of this form of what might be called corporate statism have become relatively decently off, when compared to their neoliberal cousins. These improvements in living conditions in Korea at least came to an abrupt halt with the gradual withdrawal of the state as protector of the national economy. This opened the way to full involvement in the international economy, and soon enmeshed Korea in the wider Asian financial crisis that was based on overexpansion of production and speculation. The consequent cutbacks and layoffs then triggered widespread protests and strikes.

The authoritarian nature of the state can be viewed as the "price" that an underdeveloped country must pay for domestic capital accumulation, since investment must be sweated out of the labor force that, in the absence of repression, would soon revolt. Indeed, the very success of such a regime leads to an increase in the demand for both democracy, and economic gain, hence to the organized protest movements that then take the lead when economic success fades.

In the developed "West" (including Japan), the parliamentary state also has two subdivisions. Until the mid-1970s, the liberal or social-democratic form, associated in the United States with the concept of the New Deal, appeared to be achieving dominance as the appropriate path to both profit and social control. Instead of outright repression, reform—a share of the spoils of growth—appeared to be successful in containing any serious challenge to the system. Although reformist in economics, increasing attempts to establish more authoritarian structures politically (in order to cope with large-scale protest movements such as civil rights and antiwar) have appeared, especially after economic dislocations began to increase after the mid-1970s. These forms of repression (which will be described in the next chapter) are sometimes far more sophisticated than the outright brutality characteristic of the Third World.

With increasing economic stress, a second version, sometimes labeled rhetorically as "Thatcherism," began to appear in the 1970s. This alternative strategy is enlightened in neither its economic program nor its political structure. It is capitalism with its less human face as social nets are shredded, and the poor and immigrants demonized. Both forms have profoundly authoritarian implications; they represent two separate strategies intended to accomplish the same mission: the survival of capitalism as an economic system. Which form will dominate in the next several decades is still an open question, the answer heavily dependent on the strength of political protest against the misery inflicted by the second strategy on large proportions of the population. Since the neoliberal policies that are increasingly attractive to the ruling classes of the First World are coming closer to policies that have been in place in much of the Third World since the end of World War II if not before, their cruelty is already generating resistance at least in some countries. The countries of the Second World, the former Soviet-type societies, are also being forced into the same procrustean bed, with even more devastating consequences: impoverishment of the general population, enrichment of a minority, and, in the wings, massive protest not necessarily of an enlightened kind. The ultranationalistic xenophobia of a Le Pen in France is not so different from that of some Great Russian chauvinists.

However, it is wrong to associate all forms of repression with the particular form of capitalist historical development called fascism, which is the subject of a later chapter. The term "fascism" has been sloppily applied to such nations as Chile (under the dictatorship of Pinochet), Pakistan, Iran (under both shah and ayatollah), South Africa (before the victory of the African National Congress), the Philippines (under Marcos), South Korea, Milosevic's Serbia, and a long line of others. With even less relevance and reverence for democratic forms it has been applied by segments of the Left to West Germany (before 1989), and the United States (for its treatment of black and Native American protest, and minorities and the poor in general). Applying the term "fascism" to specific situations, whether in lesser or more developed countries, simply because one can identify the use of terror tactics by the police or military that are also characteristically a part of fascist society is not helpful in understanding the roots, functions, and dynamics of the use of such tactics—even though to the victims a label may make little difference.

The Third World national security state differs from fascism most clearly in four respects:

1. While fascist movements grow, historically, in bitter opposition to the established tradition of Western rationalism and the Enlightenment, to liberalism and social democracy, in short, to what has been called "modernity," the national security state arises in a society in which those forces either never had a chance to become significant, or, if they did as part of the struggle to end colonialism (for example, against Spain in the early nineteenth century in South America), remained a minor cultural element limited to a small and often persecuted intelligentsia. The Enlightenment thinking of a liberal bourgeoisie scarcely had a chance given the domination of society by warlords, landlordism, the Catholic Church, corruption, and the relatively unrestricted influence of foreign capital. This despite the fact that many of the original liberators (Bolivar, for

example) had been deeply influenced by the spirit of the French Revolution.

2. While fascism appears at a point when the consensus of ruling capitalist elements begins to crumble, and at a juncture when the domestic economy is in total crisis (in contrast to an earlier, more successful period), the national security state arises in a situation of *permanent* crisis dominated by overwhelming dependence on foreign capital, or at best interdependence between foreign nations as consumers, and the state as guarantor of the delivery of some extractive commodity such as oil, minerals, rubber, or sugar. The crisis is characterized by massive rural and urban unemployment for long periods. However, the relatively small national bourgeoisie that is allied to international capital maintains a consensus as to national policy, a consensus that accepts restrictions on political liberty as the price for a superficial domestic tranquility that is presumed to be leading to progress. Shah Mohammed Reza Pahlavi was, after all, generally considered a modernizer, albeit an imperfect one.

3. This consensus, like fascism, excludes the masses, particularly the labor movement, from political participation (and sometimes the native bourgeoisie as well, a big mistake, as the shah found out) but unlike fascism it is rarely able to mobilize a significant plurality, not to mention a majority, into a movement on its own behalf, except for the "corporativist" kind (see below). The free election of a party openly representing a military-landlord-big bourgeois oligarchy is difficult to imagine, although there are borderline cases where oligarchic leaders have been popular. Where elections take place, fraud and coercion, combined occasionally with fake populist rhetoric, assures victory, and when that democratic facade becomes undermined, and the oligarchic state is threatened, "dirty" tactics similar to those of fascism are used to coerce the population. The "masses" are in fact the enemy of the state. More often than not, under these conditions, armed underground and guerrilla warfare is a virtually permanent feature. Fascism, in contrast, enjoys significant, and sometimes majority support from many, though never all, sectors of the population.

4. While fascism must, in the interest of its militarist-expansionist component (critical to the plunder base of its economic recovery and standard of living), seek to involve and mobilize the population in order to have sufficient numbers of enthusiastic recruits (and can indeed do so because of its immediate victories on both economic and military fronts, undergirded by massive doses of nationalistic and racist propaganda), the national security state uses terror to discourage participation in public life at most levels. If it were feasible to go to war against a foreign power (which it hardly is, given the immense resources needed just to maintain domestic order, and also given the large-scale fiscal corruption of the society and the military, which is often deeply implicated in corrupt business enterprises), it would approximate fascism. Yet another inhibiting factor is that international capital, the force behind the national security state, is unlikely to permit "it's" dictators to mobilize a domestic movement to fight a war, for such a mobilization would in the long run endanger stability, even if the war were to be won. Even worse should the war be lost (as in the "Falkland Islands" war between Argentina and Great Britain, which resulted in the overthrow of the Argentine regime then in power). And should such a dictator decide to liberate himself and his country from international capital so as to fight a war, so as to realize the nationalist rhetoric that already exists on paper, he would most likely risk economic disaster (capital flight) or military intervention in clandestine or other form to prevent such an adventure.

What are the political-economic underpinnings of the dynamic of those nations that "choose" dictatorship and repression as the state form appropriate to their class configurations? We have already mentioned the three basic interacting components of this form of political economy: *permanent crisis* (that is, deep poverty, unemployment, and fiscal chaos, accompanied by insurgency) in the context of an *international* capitalist system, with relatively *weak national capitalist* (and other) *class fractions* that "normally" produce a modern bourgeois-liberal parliamentary form of government. Perhaps this can be better understood by counterposing these dimensions to their opposites. Dale L. Johnson has written:

> The continuation of democratic forms of the state assumes strong and confident national bourgeoisies, manageable crises, and a level of class struggle by workers and other progressive forces sufficient to keep the authoritarian predispositions of the dominant class in check, but not so strong a level of class struggle as to threaten the prevailing order. The general absence of democratic states in the Third World reflects the non-existence of these conditions. Local bourgeoisies are weak, faction-ridden, and structurally subordinated to international capital; transitional or organic crises cannot be managed; and class struggle cannot be contained within the limits of the existing order....[1]

There is one widespread misconception about Third World nations that must be cleared up in this context. While it is true that national security states arise out of an epoch in which national bourgeoisies had *yet* to obtain political and ideological hegemony (in contrast to fascism, which arises *after* the collapse of the hegemony), this does not mean that this form of society or state is in any way "backward" or nonmodern. It is just as modern, as evolved, as the so-called developed or industrialized world. The problem is that its development has become distorted (away from the classical model), dependent, so that it has the *appearance* of underdevelopment, due to the abysmal poverty of most of its population (large-scale un- and underemployment, shantytowns, hunger, illiteracy, disease, crime, etc.). But that "underdevelopment" is actually the consequence of being part of the development of the global economy. It represents the development of underdevelopment, or the development of dependent development, a development that is dependent on external forces.

The full integration of dependent nations into the international economic order, which some scholars have described as "modernization," very rarely leads to a concomitant parliamentary form of government, except sometimes at the formal or rhetorical level, which is required for international propaganda purposes in order to encourage investment and discourage public outrage in the "human rights community." Rather, as Johnson has pointed out, the contrary is the case: "[T]he most 'modern' form of political rule in the Third World is military dictatorship... [and] not only in the sophisticated management of repression." This form involves

> the restructuring of the state as an efficient instrument of capital accumulation and repression of oppositional forces.... National security states are found in those nations of the Third World that have the most developed or most rapidly developing capitalisms; they occur in countries that are the most integrated into the international economy of investments by transnational corporations, international trade, and huge loans from the financial institutions of the U.S., Europe, and Japan.[2]

Nowadays this statement requires some amending. Repression increasingly takes place under civilian sponsorship behind which military power continues to guarantee that real popular participation, especially of the kind that might challenge existing economic structures, will continue to be limited.

The national security type of oligarchy can be contrasted to more traditional oligarchies, which are "merely" corrupt and brutal, but are driven by internal dynamics. In the national security state repression (the necessary price of austerity, that is, low wages and poor working conditions) takes on an international dimension, and responds to international demands.

Pakistan is a good example of the "precivilian" phase of the national security state. Six months following the inauguration of the (senior) Bhutto regime, a World Bank team met to consider Pakistan's economic crisis. It linked possible foreign aid to control of the internal labor situation, while literally at the same moment armed police were shooting striking workers in Karachi. Within two years there had been a 3,000 percent increase in budget allocations for police and intelligence services. Nevertheless, by 1975 Pakistan's foreign debt stood at $5 billion, half of which had been accumulated in the previous five years, three of which were under Bhutto. In its 1975–76 report, Amnesty International estimated that there were 38,000 political prisoners in Pakistan.

In early 1977, Saudi Arabia came forward to make up part of Pakistan's international deficit, providing a politically more stable situation was developed. At that point, First National City Bank suspended its marketing of a $300 million commercial loan, which was being backed by Iran. The shah of Iran (still in power then) announced his willingness to intervene if the situation got "out of hand." France stopped delivery of nuclear plant blueprints, and President Jimmy Carter suspended tear gas and military aircraft shipments. The situation had become "destabilized." On July 5, 1977, Bhutto, opposed by significant sectors of the upper class, which feared his minimal reform program, was overthrown by Maj. Gen. Zia Ul Haq, who initially gained fame while on loan to Jordan, where he had been one of the main commanders in the destruction of Palestinian guerrilla forces. The actual military coup was supported militarily by Iranian personnel and helicopters. At that time, the U.S. ambassador to Iran was the former head of the CIA, Richard Helms. After Zia's takeover, the Iranian ambassador to Pakistan was the man who had previously headed Iran's notorious secret service, the SAVAK. This pattern was described by the journal *Pakistan Progressive* (edited abroad) as the beginning of "an Indo-Iranian financial and military axis," which was to be linked to an "Amer-Irani axis." This of course was not to be, as the shah was overthrown in 1979 in a mass uprising led by the Ayatollah Khomeini.

By the early 1980s Pakistan had plunged into permanent crisis, with an extreme polarization of the population in both rural and urban areas: 3.5 million peasants lived on 15 percent of the land, averaging five acres each, while at the other extreme 64,000 landowners owned 30 percent of the land. This distribution was, and still is, by no means the worst in the Third World. The process has been described as follows:

> We buy capital goods, luxury items, weapons, police training, instruments of torture, technical training, etc., almost exclusively from the advanced Western countries; and we export not only raw materials and secondary goods but also great numbers of doctors, engineers and other highly qualified personnel to these same countries.... Agriculture itself has been given an export orientation, with sharp decline in quality and quantity of foodstuffs on the domestic market.... Higher incomes for the landowning classes have led either to increased conspicuous consumption and non-productive investment... or to intensified capitalization and mechanization of agriculture.... Poor peasants... sell out their farms at a time when opportunities for alternative employment and investment have contracted sharply.[3]

This description fits many Third World countries.

The role of transnational corporations, banking institutions, and the CIA in the destabilization of the reformist Allende government in Chile is by now well known. A less well-known dimension of this internationalized structure is what became known as the South Africa-FRG-Chile Triangle, the first step of what was intended to become a South Atlantic Treaty Organization. The Chilean junta under Pinochet received, in the mid-1970s, some 40 percent of its arms from (at that time) racist South Africa, most of which originated in the Federal Republic of Germany (FRG), Israel, and Great Britain. The FRG ambassador to Chile at that time, Erich Straetling, was the former FRG ambassador to South Africa. Straetling was a strong supporter of the Pinochet regime, and an advocate for "Colonia Dignidad," a German model farm in Chile that, according to Amnesty International, was used by the Chilean secret police, then called DINA, as a concentration camp and torture center. Another Pinochet supporter was Franz-Josef Strauss, then Germany's leading conservative politician. In May 1977, a West German court banned Amnesty International from further publication and distribution of its report on Colonia Dignidad in the Federal Republic, despite the existence of a 1976 UN report confirming all details; the FRG representative abstained from the vote releasing the report out of the UN's Economic and Social Council.[4] These facts were widely acknowledged and covered in the German press more than twenty years later, when the founder of Colonia Dignidad, Paul Schaefer, was being sought for sex crimes by Interpol, which was acting for both the German and Chilean governments.

Some of these accounts may seem like ancient history. However, they illustrate the fact that current events are not unprecedented, indeed have roots in the not-so-long ago past. Two arguments have appeared that seemingly put this past into perspective: one, that after all most military regimes have now been displaced by civilians; and second, that (to coin a hackneyed Stalinist phrase), you can't make an omelet without breaking eggs, that is, political repression and economic belt-tightening in the service of capital accumulation is the price for later prosperity. Neither argument holds much water empirically. The decreased frequency of outright military dictatorship tells us little about the character of the national security state, which can be more effectively run by an autocratic civilian backed by the military (as in Peru), or if not backed, then at minimum enjoying the tacit support of the military (as in Chile), or (as in Mexico) by a corrupt one-party state that is so closely interconnected with business and crime rackets that the distinction becomes irrelevant. Public relations (the "human rights" issue; the notion that civilian rule is somehow more acceptable to investors from the democratic West because it apprears to be more stable) are not compatible with direct military rule. Moreover, where the military is integrated with capital directly in the sense that high-ranking officers have large economic holdings in legitimate (or illegitimate, such as drugs) economic enterprises, that stake promotes stability and motivates military support for parliamentary regimes that tolerate such arrangements.

However, the more important debate has to do with the "omelet" question. In empirical fact, it is not true that placing harsh limitations on the civilian population will in the foreseeable future lead more broadly to a more equitable and prosperous society. What happens, with a few exceptions, is that the eggs are broken, but no omelets appear (except in the kitchens of the upper strata).

Several examples will serve as illustrations, again from Latin America, because the cases there are less complicated by the kind of complex colonial histories characteristic of either Sub-Saharan Africa or Southeast Asia.

The classical example is Chile. The argument of the "Chicago Boys," the exponents of the virtues of laissez-faire as the road to prosperity, is that the introduction of a "free market" (unencumbered by government regulation of investment, trade, or currency) will, no matter what the immediate cost (the breaking of the eggs), lead to better times (the omelet). In 1969, before the election of the reformist Allende government, 28.5 percent of the population lived in poverty. In 1979, six years after the overthrow of the Allende government and its displacement by a military junta committed to reopening the country to foreign investors, 36 percent of the population lived in poverty, despite one of the highest growth rates in the economy in all of South America, and low inflation and unemployment rates. In 1985, Chile overall consumed 15 percent less food and consumer goods than in 1970, the year Allende was elected. But the top 20 percent of the population was consuming 30 percent more, while the bottom 40 percent was consuming 50 percent less. By 1989, 42 percent of Chileans were living in poverty. Caloric intake, which is often taken to be a standard of living index, had dropped by more than 23 percent for the bottom fifth of the population. Although things have improved slightly since that time (the poverty rate was back down to 28.4 percent by 1994), the concentration of wealth at the top also increased. The head of Chile's largest conglomerate has a net worth of $2.3 billion; the top six conglomerates now own 20 percent of all capital. Even though the harsh repression of the

Pinochet years is over, the legacy of that period has sufficiently depoliticized (frightened) large sectors of the population that resistance to the impoverishment imposed by global market conditions, mediated by Chile's quasi-parliamentary state, although it exists, has yet to become significant.

Brazil is another case where a high economic growth rate is unrelated to general prosperity, contrary to conventional economic wisdom. In 1991 Brazil had the ninth largest economy in the world. Its economy was growing at a 7 to 10 percent rate per year. Yet, according to the World Bank, the gap between its rich and poor was the second largest in Latin America (after Panama's!). In a land that is still largely (though decreasingly) rural, .9 percent of landowners own 44 percent of the land, while the poorest 53 percent own just 2.7 percent. What is particularly fascinating about the case of Brazil is that President Fernando Henrique Cardoso, who was once well known as a Marxian sociologist, put into action a plan, largely conceived by the International Monetary Fund and the World Bank, that placed Brazil smack into the middle of the globalizing marketplace, which necessarily included "embracing the position of... the Brazilian business class... [and] the current international relations of power and dependency." As one of his critics put it, he has offered himself (and Brazil) as the " '*condottiere* [mercenary soldiers] of the industrial bourgeoisie,' capable of redirecting it to its manifest destiny as the lesser, dependent partner of Western capitalism. . . ."[5]

The case of Costa Rica is more illustrative in some ways because it is after all considered a democratic society and also a model of market-oriented economic development. Its economy, once largely based on agricultural exports, has since the 1960s experienced a growing "maquiladora" manufacturing sector.[6] Between 1977 and 1981 its debt quadrupled and a moratorium on payments had to be declared. But then the U.S. Agency for International Development (AID) began to provide funds because the United States was trying to build a stable showcase next door to the Sandinistas. Between 1983 and 1985 U.S. economic aid amounted to one-third of the

Costa Rican state budget, the equivalent of one-fifth of export earnings, and 10 percent of Gross Domestic Product. Even with that help, no real long-range improvement of the poverty rate took place. Between 1987 and 1991 the poverty rate increased from 18.6 percent to 24.4 percent of the population.

Intervening in, or perhaps supplementing, the globalization picture is the drug issue. Bolivia was in such dire straits that by 1985 one in eight Bolivians was dependent on foodstuffs donated by nongovernmental organizations. But by 1991 Bolivia was receiving $35.9 million in military aid and $200 million in economic aid to cope with the drug "problem." U.S. Special Forces arrived in 1991 to help in the drug "war," which is really the point: in 1987 the coca/cocaine business generated $1.4 billion, of which $500 million remained in the country: 11 percent of Bolivia's Gross Domestic Product. In that year drug exports equaled legal foreign earnings. The economic viability of Bolivia in fact rested on the drug trade. In an odd interview in Poland in 1989, laissez-faire economist Jeffrey Sachs, associated with the so-called Chicago School of "free market" economists, brought over to Poland for consultation for whatever perverse reason by the Solidarity parliamentary caucus, was asked about the prospect for the poor in Bolivia. "To tell you the truth, no one knows...if you are brave, if you are gutsy, if you do everything right, you will end up with a miserable, poor economy with stable prices," he was quoted as saying.[7] However, this "shock treatment" economic program (called, in Peru, Fujishock) has resulted in putting millions of people out of work. In a number of Latin American countries (most notoriously in Colombia) the cultivation of coca and poppies, and the industry that transforms these crops into a marketable export commodity, is the only viable source of employment for both farmers and other workers; indeed, the profits generated from drugs fuels local legitimate enterprises. The "war on drugs" is therefore futile so long as "neoliberal" economic measures prevail: if the president of the United States of America wants "free trade" he will have to accept drugs with it.

There is little evidence that foreign investment raises the real wages (purchasing power) of most workers in Third World countries, and considerable evidence of the opposite. The assumption is often that as exports to the First World increase, the profits of an "export-driven" economy will ultimately trickle down and real wages will also increase. This is true only under limited circumstances, in fact only when state intervention (as in South Korea or Singapore) regulates the economy in such a way that profit is more equitably distributed, or, in even more statist societies, where state ownership of enterprises enables the state to dispose of profits in different ways than are likely in "free market" economies, where profit is repatriated (back to the First World), and/or pocketed by a small minority of increasingly wealthy owners.

A recent study of the apparel industry in El Salvador and in Honduras, run on maquiladora principles, demonstrates that as exports increase, real wages actually decline.[8] The fact that unions are weak or nonexistent in countries that are dictatorships in all but name surely contributes to the fact that hourly wages for Honduran maquila workers hover around $0.38. As recently as September 1995 the Honduran military, which was under some pressure from human rights groups, was conducting tank maneuvers in the capital as a veiled threat to the civilian government not to go too far in pursuing past human rights violations.

In addition to low wages, dictatorial and quasi-dictatorial regimes also act to protect an extreme inequality of income and wealth, that is, they assure the increasing prosperity of the rich. Thailand, an interesting example, is a country of immense natural resources. Although primarily agricultural, it has long since ceased to be "underdeveloped." Urbanization, the pull of maquilalike factory jobs in the face of the push of rural poverty (60 percent of the population lives in rural poverty today) has turned Bangkok into a sprawling, polluted disaster area typical of many large cities in the Third World. But factory jobs have not brought prosperity. Thailand has the world's fifth most unequal distribution of income, the worst outside Latin America. In 1976 the richest 20 percent of the population received about 49 percent of all income; by 1996 it was 63 percent. Meanwhile the poorest 20 percent, which received 5 percent of all income in 1976, received even less, 3.4 percent in 1996. Thailand is a constitutional monarchy with a parliament. In a strange historical twist, the military, which is deeply involved in the private sector (as well as in contraband operations involving not only weapons but also lumber), is inhibited from simply abolishing an inefficient and often cantankerous parliament only by a throwback to feudal times, the traditional monarch, who is supported by the Buddhist clergy and deeply revered by much of the population. Yet this bad situation has become even worse. Speculation in the nonproductive real estate and financial sectors, and overproduction in the maquila industries, resulted in the collapse of the Thai currency in 1997, capital flight, vast layoffs, and widespread emiseration, as was also true of several other Asian countries that year and in the following period.

The tragic history of Haiti tells us a great deal about the relationship between dictatorship and poverty. Not so long ago, in the mid-1980s, Haiti was under the thumb of the Duvaliers, senior, then junior. Per capita income was $270, one of the world's lowest, and the unemployment rate exceeded 50 percent. The prevailing wage for those who could find work (in the maquila system mostly) was $2.65 a day. In addition to low wages (the result in large part of the fact that labor unrest was rare due to brutal suppression), the Haitian government was offering tax exemptions. American and other foreign businesses lauded Haiti as "the Taiwan of the '80s" due to its favorable climate of investment. Within a few years, some 300 foreign companies had set up shop manufacturing or assembling such products as toys (including Sesame Street figures), clothing, sports equipment, and electronics items. The long-term consequences of these miserable conditions was emigration, legal and otherwise, and, ultimately, the revolution that placed a shaky democratic regime in power, shaky for two reasons: its inability to carry through basic reforms (because the international business community would not permit it); and the continued presence of armed elements of the old order (some of which were, or had been, linked to the CIA, which had supported the Duvaliers and distrusted the reformers under Aristide who were now in power).

The history of the emergence of the national security state is complex. In some countries dependent development followed a period (mostly prior to World War II) when national bourgeoisies, aided by "their" states, often did attempt economic development intended to be independent of foreign controls. This was known as the "import substitution industrialization" model because the idea was to substitute local production for imports, thus making a nation less dependent on manufactured goods from abroad, goods paid for at disadvantageous terms by extractive commodities (agricultural or mineral). This model was often supported by large sectors of the population, and promoted by populist leaders. It led to some growth of local middle-class elements for a time. However, this native bourgeoisie was rarely fully in control, or if so only briefly, because international capital continued to be in control of large-scale investment and banking terms. Financing the process of independent development still required reliance on foreign loans. As external debt grew, interest payments grew, and financial restructuring, required by the lender nations, then undermined the model. Consquently, overall growth was limited. This form of uneven development tended to protect the most backward and traditional fractions of the landlord class, and held back the development of a genuine national bourgeoisie rooted in industrial capital. At the same time, this limitation was often accompanied by the development of a middle stratum of managers of private and public enterprise that was imbued with the values of consumerism associated with the outside world. That is, segments of the population became victims of what is called "cultural imperialism." This stratum was fearful of mass movements, hence tended to be politically conservative, and fought against those populist leaders who threatened from time to time to "unleash" the masses.

The "problem," so to speak, for the lender nations was to construct a way of making that part of the bourgeoisie that was tied to international capital dominant politically, that is, decisive in decision making at the state level, at the expense of other fractions and most certainly at the expense of the working class and poor peasantry. The way this was often done was to forge an alliance between some fractions of the bourgeoisie and the military, and then to create an unstable political situation that made military intervention possible and successful. Often success was helped along by the CIA contributing to the destabilization of reform-type governments, as in Guatemala, Indonesia, or Chile. Following a military overthrow of a nationally oriented and reform-minded bourgeois government, multinational corporations and the military come to dominate the state, and dependent development (or the development of underdevelopment, another way of expressing it) proceeds.

However, since the class base of the state is fairly narrow, more and more repressive measures are required, hence the term "national security state." Security becomes the key to survival because dependent development generates permanent crisis (vast inequities in income and wealth, emiseration of large sectors of the population, constant outbursts of resistance). Seething unrest at all levels of the society, masked only by superior military force, is constant.

Under the first Bhutto regime in Pakistan there were no industrial centers where arrest and torture did not take place on a widespread scale, where police did not occupy union offices, where militants were not massacred. In Baluchistan in January 1977, 100,000 soldiers were deployed in a complete military occupation intended to subdue strikes. In Brazil, a coup instituted a "state of exception" (the common term for suspending the constitution) in April 1964. In Bolivia a "state of siege" (another term for suspension of civil rights and liberties) was declared following a coup in 1978. In Nicaragua, where the ruling family owned one-fourth of all the arable land in the country, the Sandinista movement began an insurrection in 1978 that succeeded in overthrowing the Somoza regime despite every effort by the U.S. government to prevent it. In Iran, the shah's regime, also supported and indeed installed by the United States, was overthrown after several years of widespread unrest and massive demonstrations and strikes. In Guatemala, a reform government was overthrown by the military, aided by the CIA, in 1954. A bitter, brutal civil war that ended with a truce only in late 1996 ensued. Problems do not cease by decree, nor does the displacement of one dictator by another on the ground that the successor will "save" the country from chaos or leftist revolution work for very long. The basic crisis of the economic and social dislocations flowing inevitably from typical Third World class configurations in the context of an international economy remains, as we see in Chiapas, Mexico, even today.

A country-by-country report on the state of human rights in national security states would be superfluous. Each year's Amnesty International report catalogues the situation. It might be well to keep in mind, however, that in the formative postwar decades from 1945 to about 1977 the United States sent well more than $140 billion in aid to Third World countries, nearly two-thirds of which went to governments that were, in the words of a Center for International Policy draft report, then "flagrantly violating universally recognized human rights," including $13.5 billion to South Korea, $5.5 billion to Brazil, $3 billion to Iran, the same amount to Indonesia and the Philippines, and over $60 billion in all to Guatemala, Argentina, Nicaragua, Taiwan, Zaire, Chile, Uruguay, Ethiopia, Haiti (all dictatorships at the time), and various others. In 1979, fifteen of the world's most repressive governments received $2.9 billion in World Bank loans, or almost one-third of all loans. "The reason," says the CIP report, "...is the willingness of their new military rulers to impose World Bank–approved economic policies."[9] And pretty much in vain on two grounds: this aid has not led to "modernization," if by that is meant a rising standard of living for most people, better education, a growing middle class, and genuinely democratic structures; and it has not led to stability either, for with the exception perhaps of Taiwan in the above list, coups, revolutions, civil war, or (at minimum) constant mass unrest has characterized all these countries.

Lest it be imagined that the concept of the national security state was invented by its critics, we turn now to a brief description of the ideology of that form of state, as explicitly expressed in Brazil. The Brazilian coup of April 1964, which put an end to the moderate progress, democratic evolution, and agrarian reform of the previous regime, was based on a theory officially termed the Doctrine of National Security. This "Doctrine" had been, according to Jean-Louis Weil (in a report submitted to a Bertrand Russell Tribunal concerning war crimes), developed in the Higher College of War (in Brazil) in the 1950s. The foundation of this doctrine rests on three assumptions: (1) that hegemony over Southern Atlantic Latin America would rest in Brazilian hands, in turn backed by the United States; (2) that it is justified by "the necessity for development which can only be assured by absolute order and undivided power"; and (3) that any forces that would interfere with this program would be eliminated. Thus "the goal was to neutralize all opinions contrary to this plan and to define as an internal enemy anyone opposing the military dictatorship...."[10]

The pattern of defining political opposition in criminal terms is characteristic of all national security states, indeed of all totalitarian states. It is promoted first as a fact of life. Then, typically, a series of decrees is promulgated that in effect transforms the constitution into a government under a "state of siege." In this manner, the "exceptional state" quickly becomes the normal state.

Under a 1969 Brazilian decree, for example, every person was answerable to "national security," which was defined to include "the prevention and repression of hostile psychological warfare and revolutionary or subversive warfare (including)...hostile threats or pressures, of whatever origin, of whatever shape or kind, which are manifest or have an effect in the country...propaganda or counter-propaganda and any activity...which aims at influencing or producing opinions, emotions, attitudes and actions...."[11]

The decree further banned workplace meetings, the formation of committees, public meetings, marches, demonstrations, strikes, insult, calumny or defamation of public authorities, and allows detention of up to thirty days with denial of communication up to ten days prior to trial. The practice of criminalizing the act of "insulting" public figures and the practice of detention incommunicado are common to all forms of modern dictatorship as well as to states that are ostensibly democratic, for example, the Federal Republic of Germany (see the next chapter), and Israel, which has more recently come under international scrutiny.

In the context of relatively weak domestic bourgeois elements, the military plays a very important role and sometimes develops its own internal factions, some of which see themselves as repositories of national pride and independence. That is, some factions take the ideology of national security seriously, and accept an internal ideological logic that drives that doctrine, given its hegemonistic geopolitical dimension, to the edge of, or over into, fascist ideology. Comblin has argued that geopolitics (in the Pan-German, Nazi sense) is inherent in national security doctrine, and that the logic of Brazilian geopolitics at least at one time was to dominate a geographical space much akin to the demands of Hitler's Germany for expansion into the European "heartland"—the so-called *Lebensraum* doctrine.

This has occasionally led to military adventurism, as when Argentina went to war against Britain in the Falklands. But this ideology runs counter to the interests of multinational corporations. It is a destabilizing influence in the region hardly in the interest of a stable international market.

The doctrine of national security involves several important contradictions: (1) Internal security violates the strivings of those fractions of the bourgeoisie traditionally committed to a modern, Western European tradition: republics within which those fractions can effectively contest for domination and express themselves personally (individualistically) without fear; (2) In a society in which the overwhelming majority of the population is poor, and excluded from all effective political participation, constant unrest is virtually inevitable, even if it can be temporarily contained by brute force; (3) the nationalist doctrine of some of the military, supported by some segments of the newer (state-based) bourgeoisie, endangers regional peace, hence constitutes a challenge to the multinational corporations that seek integration among nations (not excluding hegemony by one nation) but not at the price of war or the danger of war (with the instability that such danger poses—including the possibility of coup or revolution succeeding war).

The vulnerability of the national security state to coup, countercoup, fascist coup, or, at the other extreme, breakdown and revolution, or even the establishment, by legal means, of a democratic state by an antioligarchic alliance that includes the republican bourgeoisie plus the repressed organizations of workers and peasants, is therefore obvious. It is also obvious to a dictatorship, hence its continuing cruelties.

Yet the politics that accompany the globalization of the marketplace frown on overt brutality. It becomes more and more important to legitimate the hegemony of the international economy in the eyes of populations whose at least tacit support is needed to "man" the labor force, or at minimum not to be overly disruptive. The "human rights" movements both challenge and legitimate the global marketplace. They challenge because they question the human price that is paid for cheap labor: the suppression of labor organizations, prison, torture. They legitimate because insofar as they are successful, the overt cruelties of dictatorships are softened and even replaced by quasi-parliamentary institutions, although the exploitation of labor continues, albeit at a less oppressive level. The basic rules of the game are reformed, but the game continues.

One other factor in this equation is a gradual shift of power from more traditional landed oligarchies to more modern, business oligarchies. To some extent, at least, these more modern capitalists (who are oriented to the global marketplace and have more transnational links both economically and culturally) prefer civilian regimes, as in Peru. Anyway, it is no longer really necessary to have direct military control because in today's multinational world, dictatorships to subdue mass movements take second place to multinational capital's ability to impose rules that themselves force populations to tighten their belts. It is preferable under these new circumstances to have a democratically elected government impose those rules rather than to have dictators do it, as in the past. It is harder to resist a "soft" or "friendly" dictatorship than a harsh one. Moreover, it is increasingly evident that national governments can truthfully say that those rules are beyond their control anyway. One observer put it this way:

> As the multilaterals [the World Bank and the International Monetary Fund] become proxy governments, and transnational banking institutions become truly global, being the president of, say, Mexico has become much like being the mayor of Detroit. And soon, being the head of a national bank like, say, Mexico's Banamex, will be like being a branch manager of Fleet Bank in Poughkeepsie, N.Y. Wolfensohn and Camdessus [president of the World Bank and managing director of the IMF] are just telling it like it is: national governments and financial systems—especially in Latin America—have been weakened, perhaps beyond repair. The stability and legitimacy of profitmaking are now global responsibilities. So meet the new State. Same as the old state. Just a little bit bigger.[12]

The "perfected" national security state would be one in which a comparatively weak national bourgeoisie is not capable of ruling and is not allowed to rule, and an internationally oriented oligarchy, working in close alliance with multinational businesses and their respective states, utilizes a military dictatorship in order to dominate the society. In real life, there are today few clear-cut cases of this kind. There are, rather, many states with varying degrees of participation by local bourgeoisies in "their" state, varying levels of mass participation, different degrees of direct military involvement, and gradations of integration with or control by outside forces.

Historically, Bonapartist dictatorships and quasi-dictatorships have acted as bridges to the development of strong national bourgeoisies. Even though such new bourgeoisies in time become integrated into the world market, it has in the past been as fairly independent, rather than dependent junior, partners. Such an independent development is no longer possible.

Iran is an example of a *failed* Bonapartist dictatorship. Shah Mohammed Reza Pahlavi overthrew a reformist parliamentary state that had nationalized the oil industry, and resumed full power in 1953 with the assistance of the CIA. Ruling with the iron hand of his secret police, the SAVAK, instead of basing himself on the mass support of the peasantry as is more typical of classical Bonapartism, the shah attempted to turn Iran into a modern and independent capitalist power using oil as a weapon. However, his modernization from above alienated not only peasants dislocated by his land-reform program (which favored agribusiness), but also a growing underemployed intelligentsia and, even more important, a large, religiously conservative petty-bourgeoisie of merchants. The shah's modernization program became identified with Westernization, including such modernist ideas as the desegregation of the genders. The consequence was an antimodernist backlash, resulting in the overthrow of the shah and the creation of a Muslim state in 1979. This despite continuing support of the shah by the U.S. government until the very end. (The CIA subsequently collaborated with the new ruler, Khomeini, aiding him in his efforts to expunge the Left from Iranian politics.)

The major influence of the state in the shah's modernization effort suggests a label for this form of national security state: state capitalism (the state as capitalist in partnership with capitalism, and as promoter of capitalism, but not the state as capitalist in order to monopolize capital, as in Communism). In this context, what is the current Iranian regime? The Khomeini revolution reversed the progress women had made under the shah, but it also renationalized banks and most industry that was not already state-owned. It also opened the door wider to foreign investment, thereby negating its revolutionary, anti-Western rhetoric in practice. The term "Theo-Bonapartism" would not be far-fetched, since the Iranian Islamic "republic" must necessarily be a bridge to something else. It is creating its own gravediggers as a native bourgeoisie and intelligentsia grows to perform intermediary functions for Iran in the global marketplace.

A number of newly independent nations have chosen a state capitalist-oriented form of Bonapartism, with little success. Authoritarian modernization without real gains for the general population has generated antimodernist movements that have proven troublesome at best, as in Turkey, and have led to virtual civil war conditions at worst, as in Algeria.

The exceptions are in Asia: Singapore, Taiwan, and especially South Korea. "South Korea's economic growth and industrial transformation," Hart-Landsberg concludes, "was largely the result of highly centralized and effective state planning and direction of economic activity."[13] Following a military coup in 1961, the state, under a series of military dictators, suppressed labor while promoting the "Chaebol," family-business conglomerates created to exploit labor and develop an export-oriented economy. The long-term result was that by 1980 South Korea enjoyed a per capita income twice that of Honduras, Nicaragua, El Salvador, or Peru. But the political consequence is that the very success of this planning model has led to the growth of opposition movements demanding basic rights. In December 1996, strikes protesting laws allowing employers more leeway about layoffs hit a high point. The economy was slowing down. Jobs were being lost to lower-wage areas of Asia. Increasing crisis for Korea as the state drew back from the interventionist model, and allowed the Chaebol to move toward a "free market" economy, became likely. By 1997, following more deregulated conditions that permitted expanded borrowing from international financial institutions, speculation took off. Risky ventures failed to pay off, and loans defaulted. There was a run on banks, and a wave of bankruptcies, accompanied by layoffs, followed. Korea's crisis became joined to that of other Asian countries, all suffering from an overeagerness to open themselves to unregulated international investment. This crisis has even affected "Communist" China and Vietnam, which have sought and found capitalist investors, have overexpanded production, and are now forced to cut labor costs in order to offer cheap goods on the world market in competition with other low-wage countries.

Whatever the future may hold, it is clear that the Korean success story was not due to "neoliberal" free-market policies. Quite the contrary: Korean Bonapartism had promoted a powerful national capitalist class from the top, by planning. The future of that class is an open question.

Classical Bonapartism of the kind described by Marx does not exclude mass participation. Indeed, it rests on a mass base, the peasantry, even as it peforms the function of creating the prerequisites for the development of a bourgeoisie, and the emiseration of the peasants and their replacement with agribusiness. It utilizes populist, antiurban, and nationalist rhetoric. Military personnel are often drawn from the lower strata and officers moving up through the ranks may play leading roles in the Bonapartist project. In Mexico, the Institutional Revolutionary Party (PRI) completely dominated the state from the early 1930s until very recently. It combined a Bonapartist framework of populist rhetoric with promoting capitalist economic development, but also including some land redistribution, nationalization of oil, and other popular reforms, although these programs were always vulnerable to political wheeling and dealing.

Sociologist James D. Cockcroft terms this kind of state "corporativism," which he defines as "a political system that relies for its legitimacy and perpetuation on a politics of masses, where the capitalist state provides modest concessions to popular movements and ties their mass organizations to its tutelage and where those resisting such incorporation are usually repressed by state force." Organizations ranging from peasant and labor unions to professional and business groups represent fractions of several classes, and insofar as they are tied to the PRI, they mobilize support for it (and its state), but are also able to extract concessions within the larger capitalist project. This populist structure provided legitimacy for "the consolidation of dependent state monopoly-capitalism" by around 1970, a structure that was to lead to "continued economic dependence on the United States and to an ever greater maldistribution of income and social benefits."[14] This was the context not only for fiscal crisis, as Mexico became more indebted, but also for increasing unrest and the growth of militant opposition.

There are therefore several subtypes of the national security state. It can still take the form, even at this point at the brink of the twenty-first century, of an outright oligarchic dictatorship of the Pinochet kind. Or it can approximate a corporativist form with a populist flavor, as in Mexico. There have been national indepence or anticolonial revolutions, as in Egypt or Tunisia, where army officers or revolutionary leaders take the helm of such a corporativist state. Alternatively, it may take the form of a state-directed capitalism of the Korean type. Each form of state faces a common dilemma: the need to improve living standards in order to avert massive social dislocations, even revolutions (particularly in states that have arisen as the result of revolutions, and revolutionary promises), versus the reality that the capital required for development has strings attached, perhaps even chains, those imposed by the present structure of the world economy. That structure has traditionally required, and in the main still requires the opposite of free, independent national development: one that imposes belt-tightening as a condition for loans, and cheap labor as a condition for investment. So each state of what is now called the "emerging market" area of the world finds itself competing with every other one in a scramble to provide the best investment opportunity, and the optimal demonstration of willingness to conform to the rules of the international financial community.

As capitalism gradually develops, whether under one or another form of sponsorship, the classes typical of a capitalist economy also develop. Native bourgeois and professional fractions grow, as does the industrial and services sector proletariat. Small-scale farming declines; peasants become urbanized and often marginalized into slums. The polarization of classes becomes more extreme. Direct dictatorship becomes more difficult to sustain in the spotlight of international media coverage. Economies built on corruption, drugs, and gangsterism become hindrances to globalization. Stability demands that states assume a friendlier and more efficient face. Old-fashioned dictators who resist are expelled and exiled. Yet those who replace them continue to face the same issue: increasing numbers of impoverished people at one end of the spectrum who outnumber by many multiples the rich and almost rich at the other, all vulnerable to a shaky global financial structure that exists only for profit. Up to this point, all efforts to cast that structure off and create one that would seriously take up the challenge of poverty, illiteracy, disease, and in addition do it utilizing democratic forms of the state have failed.

## NOTES

1. Dale Johnson, unpub. ms. (Johnson is the coauthor, with James D. Cockcroft and Andre Gunder Frank, of *Dependence and Underdevelopment* (Garden City, N.Y.: Doubleday, 1972), and numerous other works associated with "dependency theory."
2. Ibid.
3. *Pakistan Progressive* (May–June 1978).
4. Konrad Ege and Martha Wenger, "Colonia Dignidad: The Embassy of the Federal Republic of Germany and Torture in Chile" (Washington: D.C. Area Clergy and Laity Concerned, 1978, mimeographed).
5. Jose Luiz Fiori, "Cardoso among the Technopols," *Report on the Americas* 28, no. 6 (May–June 1995): 18.
6. "Maquiladora" is generally defined as a plant in the "Third World" engaged in the assembly of components manufactured elsewhere, the entire product then to be exported for sale in the "First World." The

maquila is a "branch plant" either owned directly by a First World corporation, or a subcontractor entirely dependent on an outside corporation. The maquila is labor-intensive, employing disproportionally unskilled, female, low-paid, non-union labor. More recently the definition has been extended to full production rather than only assembly, but with similar working conditions. Typical products include garments and electronic goods such as TVs. The concept "sweatshop" is not exactly synonymous. A "sweatshop" is simply any factory that violates one or more labor laws, such as the requirement to pay minimum wages, pay for overtime, not using child labor, maintaining minimum safety conditions, etc. Therefore, while all maquilas are sweatshops, not all sweatshops are maquilas.

7. Lawrence Weschler, "Bolivia Goes East," *Report on the Americas* 25, no. 1 (July 1991): 28.

8. Karen McCormack, Ellen Rosen, and Robert J. S. Clark, "Global Capitalism and the New Sweatshop" (paper presented at the Eastern Sociological Society, Boston, March 31, 1996).

9. Center for International Policy, "U.S. Aid, Foreign Policy, and Repressive Regimes" (report prepared for Human Rights Organizing Conference, October 1–2, 1977).

10. Jean Louis Weil, "Brazil 1976: Political Prisoners and the State of Exception," in *The Repressive State*, ed. by Jean Louis Weil, Joseph Comblin, and Judge Senese (Toronto: Brazilian Studies Documents, 1976).

11. Joseph Comblin, "The National Security Doctrine," in ibid.

12. Fred Rosen, "I.M.F.: One Step Closer to a Global State," *Report on the Americas* 30, no. 3 (November–December 1996): 5.

13. Martin Hart-Landsberg, *The Rush to Development: Economic Change and Political Struggle in South Korea* (New York: Monthly Review Press, 1993), 15.

14. James D. Cockcroft, *Mexico, Class Formation, Capital Accumulation, and the State* (New York: Monthly Review Press, 1983), 139, 209. See also his *Corporativist Roots of the Modern State, 1920–1940* (New York: Monthly Review Press, 1998).

# 3

# "FRIENDLY FASCISM"?

**"F**riendly Fascism"[1] is shorthand for the idea that modern industrialized democratic nations are on the road to the establishment of repressive, authoritarian societies with some of the trappings of fascism or Stalinism, or both. There are many versions of this Orwellian outlook, ranging from the conservative Friedrich Hayek's *The Road to Serfdom*[2] or James Burnham's *The Managerial Revolution*[3] to such left-wing thinkers as Herbert Marcuse in *One-Dimensional Man*[4] or the work of the German "Frankfurt School" theorists Max Horkheimer and Theodor Adorno in their well-known work *Dialectic of Enlightenment*.[5]

Most of these approaches are deeply pessimistic. They are undialectical in the sense that they disregard or underplay the potential role of oppositional or dissenting forces, both within the establishment (from different fractions of capital) and outside. On the Left, they are often linked to a pessimism that stems from the weakening of such outsider social movements as labor and civil rights, but also from an analysis of power structures that often leaves one with a sense of hopelessness, given what appears to be the virtually monolithic power of our ruling circles. This view is also linked to both

Marxian and anarchist theories of the state. The former sees the state as an instrument that mediates among the fractions of capital and assures the survival of the system, and is therefore prepared to exert whatever force is necessary to suppress revolution, even, when necessary, by turning to fascism; the latter sees the state itself as inherently oppressive. Neither quarrel with the idea that under late capitalism, given its technological capabilities, intensified social control by the state is possible and, in a crisis situation, highly probable.

These are minority views within the broader literature of what "Western" society (normally including post–World War II Japan) is all about. The majority of thinkers, though hardly utopian, still celebrate the accomplishments of modern capitalism and look forward to a better future. The era of class struggle is over, they often say. Social problems can be resolved through technical means. Rational, scientific thought is in the ascendancy. Mass movements are, thankfully, of the past. It is, in Daniel Bell's words, *The End of Ideology.*[6] This view is shared by many liberals and mainstream social democrats who have seen their electoral base erode, and have moved toward the political center. It is a perspective that is empirically supported by the fact that there has been widespread improvement of living standards for majorities of the population in many Western countries since World War II. Yet accompanying these accomplishments (often won only after bitter struggles) has been what the skeptics, not to mention the pessimists, consider a decline in many kinds of freedom. Moreover, the improvements of the past fifty years have stalled, and much of the world never shared them anyway. Social problems are myriad and are encroaching ever more even in the citadels of Western European reformist societies.

The "friendly fascism" model in modern society, specifically in the "First World," differs significantly from the other forms of state that have been and will be described: the Bonapartist or quasi-Bonapartist states of the "Third World" that were discussed in chapter 2, fascism (chapter 5), and the former Stalinist states in the "Second World" (chapter 6). Proponents of the "friendly fascism" idea regardless of the particular term used ("garrison state" representing only one of many synonyms), and regardless of their political perspectives (which range from ultraright to ultraleft) agree in not accepting the celebratory assumptions of the status quo, and in denying the allegedly benign behavior of the state. But Right and Left disagree about the causes for this development. For conservative critics of the modern state, the social reform apparatus itself is the cause: bureaucracy grows, octopuslike, to enslave us. The solution, if one is at all possible, is to dis-integrate (downsize) the state. For leftist critics, the imminent cause is incipient crisis. As Ralph Miliband, the British socialist scholar, put it some years ago,

> The point is not that "bourgeois democracy" is imminently likely to move towards old-style fascism. It is rather that advanced capitalist societies are subject to strains more acute than for a long time past, and that their inability to resolve these strains make their evolution towards more or less pronounced forms of conservative authoritarianism more rather than less likely.[7]

However, if it is true that Western society is moving toward authoritarianism, a view that is still in dispute, there are two other questions that must be dealt with concerning the brand of authoritarianism: is it indeed conservative as Miliband thought, or is it, as many writers have contended, a liberal or even social democratic authoritarianism?

More than fifty years ago the political scientist Harold Lasswell attempted to describe the "probable" emergence of a military state under modern technological conditions, in his groundbreaking essay "The Garrison State."[8] Approaching this issue from the perspective of the sociology of elites, Lasswell argued that "specialists on violence" would surface as the dominant group in society. He came to some startling, and for that time prescient, conclusions: First, that in a garrison state "there must be a deep and general sense of participation" if morale problems were to be avoided. Hence the importance of the manipulation of symbols. (Advertising?) Second, there must be work for all, if necessary by compulsion. (Workfare?) Third, there would be government by plebiscite, with opposition parties banned, despite the continuation of the outer symbols of democracy. (Polls? The exclusion of third parties from realistic electoral participation?) Fourth, all organized social activity would be governmentalized, and highly centralized. Fifth, in the interest of morale there would be some moderation of income differences, and the rate of production would be regularized by planning. Finally, while the garrison state would be one of battle potential, with military men playing a leading role, actual violence would more likely be directed at internal than at external enemies, particularly the potentially troublesome unskilled, and suspicious elements among intellectuals.

While this description fits that of many discussions of "totalitarianism" in some respects, Lasswell's point of departure is his view that this development held for Western, democratic societies, at least potentially. Intensive governmental intervention in the economy to the point of nationalization of some industries in a country like Britain, and the significant move toward lessening economic inequality especially in the social-democratic societies of Western Europe after the war, seemed to fit with Lasswell's description. In the 1960s and 1970s, states such as West Germany and the United States also engaged in considerable internal repression of a "military" kind.

However, Lasswell's model obscured significant differences between, first, the dynamics of the two totalitarian states most under discussion at the time, Hitler's Germany and Stalin's Soviet Union; and second, the differences between both and the kinder, gentler states of Western Europe, all of which after all had, and still have, significant opposition parties with deeply rooted democratic traditions. This error was shared by other writers: Burnham's *Managerial Revolution*, published in that same year, 1941, tried to group together such fundamentally different societies as the United States under the New Deal, Germany, and the USSR, based on what Burnham saw as a similarity of planning and management forms. And the theory failed to predict the turn away from social spending and government intervention that we associate with "Reaganism" and "Thatcherism." Finally, the view that repression would be primarily violent in nature underestimated the importance of the manipulation of ideology.

Even European totalitarianism had gone beyond sheer brute violence in attaining and maintaining power, as students of propaganda well knew. But propaganda was only the tip of the iceberg. It was the social psychological front more broadly understood that became the focus, a few years later, of the German "Frankfurt School" of critical theory.

Horkheimer and Adorno, in their *Dialectic of Enlightenment*, argued that social progress itself had led to its opposite: "...the evolution of the machine has already turned into that of the machinery of domination...successful progress [is] its contrary. The curse of irresistible progress is irresistible regression."[9] Horkheimer and Adorno saw this as rooted in the psychic realm, in the problem of what happens to the human consciousness in the era of commodity fetishism and mass society. What is dialectical about this is that progress leads to its opposite: science, the prime product of the Enlightenment, leads almost inevitably to Auschwitz and the H-bomb.

It was Marcuse who explored the manipulatory forms of repression most thoroughly. Totalitarianism, he wrote, "is not only a terroristic political coordination of society, but also a non-terroristic economic-technical coordination which operates through the manipulation of needs by vested interests."[10] This works by implanting the need for commodities which in turn requires us to toil, to compete aggressively, and ultimately to exploit others. This process continues because people become incapable of distinguishing false from real needs given the degree of cultural manipulation in the society. Even more dangerous are the cultural modes of relaxation that arrest individual development. It is here that his famous notion of "repressive desublimation" comes in. It means that modern society provides freedoms that maintain the overall repressive system rather than generating challenges to it. The most important of these freedoms is in the sexual arena, where we are permitted a controlled, liberalized sexuality that does not truly liberate. Liberties that strengthen repression are granted: we enjoy music, film, drugs, sex, but in such a limited and commercialized way that we become in effect coopted. Light entertainment displaces "the critical dimensions of art, literature, music, and philosophy."[11] We become what we own, we are our commodities. And all this without violence.

Yet Marcuse's pessimism was contradicted even in his own time by the very fact that the worldwide student Left organized in part around his ideas. His analysis, as Brad Rose points out, was based on an assumption of the expanded role of the welfare state. But conservative forces bent on pauperizing the population have rolled back the welfare state in a number of countries and the cooptative potential of increasing access to commodities may be at an end. As more and more people lack the means for repressive desublimation, is it not conceivable that the ideology of consumerism will suffer as well? In which case manipulation will not suffice, and more direct forms of repression will have to be introduced, as indeed they are in the form of prison construction.

Nevertheless, Marcuse pointed to a very important dimension of repression, namely that the cultural apparatus of the society can take "steps to prevent hostile ideas and organizations from forming as an alternative to repressing them politically once they have already formed."[12] As Alan Wolfe went on to argue, when existing power relationships are based on inequality and on the exploitation of the majority by a minority, "some form of repression will always be needed, whether it be the manipulation of ideology or the use of state violence."[13] It is only a question of which form, and in what proportions.

The modern national security state, using both ideological (cultural) and violent (police) forms of repression, still differs from classical fascism even though fascism also uses both forms (in a much more extreme way). First, friendly fascism develops out of liberalism or social democracy, rather than in fundamental opposition to the liberal-left tradition, as does real fascism. It combines a still extensive, even though contested, system of social security and welfare-state practice (at least outside the United States) with a system of political "security," that is, social control of deviant cultural and political behavior (especially cultural in the United States). It speaks with the voice of the Enlightenment, rather than with the demagogy of irrationality and racial chauvinism.

Second, it appears when capitalism is threatened economically (e.g., by falling productivity, negative trade balances, inflation, growing unemployment, the growth of an "underclass," threats to profitability—all of which are of course interrelated), or when the perception of a potential for such a threat begins to develop among elites. There exist threats, or the perception of threats, from strikes, underemployed and disaffected university graduates, growing numbers of criminals, immigrants, economic competition from other nations, drugs, etc., etc. Yet the system is not actually *in* crisis, that is, at the point of collapse, as measured by really large-scale unemployment, a crisis in financial markets, the incapacity of government to function, extreme polarization of the population into Right and Left (both of which wings are politically mobilized), and the like, as is the case when fascism makes its bid for power. Corresponding to the moderate level of actual crisis, there continues to be a relatively high degree of consensus as to national policy on the part of most fractions of capital as well as the leadership of the labor movement, which by and large cooperates in measures intended to cope with economic problems in the short run (so much so that most "labor" or "socialist" parties are barely distinguishable from parties of the center, especially once they form governments).

Third, this consensus includes a large majority of public opinion. Hence the forms of parliamentary democracy, the existence of free labor unions, and even, within limits, the right to criticize the consensus decisions, are maintained. In fact, there is considerable debate within the major parties and within the power structure as well, as to the tactics by which to carry out the policies that represent the consensus. This debate hinges not on what must be done, but how much, and particularly on the proportions of the state's income that should be expended on social versus political (and military) security: schools or prisons? Inflation control or job creation? Free trade or tariffs? Tight immigration controls or loose? And in a broader sense, ideological versus police repression? Carrot or stick?

Finally, while the new national security state is characterized by lack of much opposition, it is correspondingly characterized by a considerable amount of apathy and cynicism, a lack of real mass involvement in the political process, a decline of what is called "civil society." Whatever genuine grass-roots activity exists is either coopted by foundations or by the state, that is, made harmless, or it is isolated and killed off by denial of funding, political smear campaigns, or outright police harassment and repression. The apathy and cynicism of many people toward the political process stems in part from the depolitization of issues as decisions become more and more defined as a matter for experts, and "politics" becomes the celebration of celebrities and the expose of their scandals. Stories of corruption, both financial and sexual, further deepen public apathy. The media determine the limits of what can be discussed, and define what the issues are, and just as important, what views are outside the range of acceptable dialogue. The choice of options decreases, and the "Left-Right" spectrum shifts so that center becomes defined as Left. The real Left finds itself more and more marginalized. Those who challenge the prevailing rules are often psychiatrized (labeled nuts), even as bizarre behavior becomes fodder for mass entertainment on television, and ever more bizarre figures dominate the radio airwaves with shock racist and sexist "commentary."

What are the dynamics of the relatively "clean," as opposed to the "dirty," Third World oligarchic state, or the fascist state? The modern state apparatus contains mechanisms that under the most neutral of circumstances drive it toward rationalization and integration, and toward coordination of its separate subapparatuses, what the Nazis called *Gleichschaltung*. These "neutral" mechanisms have to do with the way all bureaucracies work, and are related to the factors of size, and the kind of hierarchy and division of labor that Max Weber long ago described as inherent in all bureaucratic structures, whether capitalist, communist, fascist, or any other system, and whether benign or evil.[14]

But of course there are no neutral circumstances, since all states are obedient to class dynamics. Since the mid-1970s, the creeping economic crisis of capitalism (alleviated periodically by sporadic upturns that breed the illusion that there is no crisis) has accelerated the drive toward bureaucratic rationalization due to periodic budget shortfalls, what O'Connor has called "the fiscal crisis of the state."[15]

Despite the rhetoric of the "free market" economists and politicians, the fact is that the state's role in all modern economies has been growing. The increasingly international nature of economic relations means that this role must necessarily grow even more, since the state must take on the role of mediator between its nationally based capitalist class and other states and their capitalist classes, as all of these national capitalisms become ever more transnational and compete, or collaborate, as the case may be, across national boundaries. Budgetary shortfalls and increasing deficits, caused by a combination of inequitable and inadequate tax structures and the growing need of the state to intervene in fiscal matters and provide services as the economy weakens, lead to the promotion of a politics of austerity, and the development of a series of measures that promote rationalization in the interest of "efficiency" and savings. In addition, or perhaps even more importantly, corporations have become politically more powerful as the labor movement has weakened (a vicious cycle in which one feeds into the other), so that state policy favors profit. This translates programmatically into lower taxes, less regulation, the privatization of traditional public-sector functions, and pressure on the public sector to cut costs. Some cost-cutting means, such as increased resistance to unions and more use of part-time or "contingent" labor, are borrowed from the private sector. The Lasswellian view that the "garrison state" will be one in which income differences will decline, and state planning on the social-democratic model will prevail, has proven illusory.

One strategy that allegedly contributes to economizing is the trend toward the measurement of productivity in the formerly exempt "soft" services. The slogan of "accountability," the introduction of a series of management gimmicks (the latest of which is "Total Quality Management," or TQM for short) even in the public sector, is accompanied by the availability of cheaper sources of labor due to the growth of unemployment. Welfare recipients are forced into low-level employment including in the public sector, where they displace better-paid employees, thereby saving money and reducing taxes. Although displacement of higher-paid full-time professional labor by lower-paid and sometimes lesser-qualified part-timers no doubt does save money in the short run (at the expense of the quality of services), it is debatable as to whether management gimmicks save money at all, or whether their function is actually tighter discipline of the labor force regardless of the cost factor.

Note that only resources devoted to the development and enhancement of human services come under attack as wasteful, while those oriented to the management or control of the population (for example, the "criminal justice system") expand. Military expenditures also continue to increase. The "reserve army of labor," the unemployed and the underemployed, grows as manufacturing jobs move to areas and countries with lower labor costs, and as technological improvements in productivity displace other workers, pushing social costs (unemployment compensation, welfare) up. Insofar as new jobs are created, large proportions of them are at the lower end of the labor force, in the services sector, and pay little. As workers become less able to pay taxes due to lower wages and unemployment, local governments become less able to support their infrastructures (especially educational plant and health care), resulting in populations less educated, and less healthy, hence less capable of taking their places in the increasingly technology-driven economy.

Public resources, at both local and larger state levels, are unable to cope with the combination of human needs and political graft (subsidies to agribusiness, the military, and other forms of direct or indirect graft), and then the "costly welfare apparatus" is advertised as diverting state resources from the encouragement of investment.

One measure of "success" in the drive toward savings by means of accountability measurement is the appearance of unity within an organization. Public display of criticism becomes suppressed. Allocation of funds is linked to the suppression of deviant views and the promotion of loyalty. One result is the degradation of professional ethics, the suppression of "whistle-blowing," and the general relegation of qualitative issues to the unspeakable, while decisions are made more and more on quantitative (measurable) bases. The trend toward mass production and profit in the movement toward "managed" health care (which is being increasingly protested) is an example, as is the trend toward "objective" testing for all sorts of jobs. One could argue that radicals are wrong in concentrating on the activities of the CIA—it is the Educational Testing Service in Princeton they should be worried about, as education becomes more skewed toward test preparation and less toward critical thinking, civic values, or other more traditional orientations.

The measurement of output units (whether clients, patients, students, or any other public sector "product") contributes to the depoliticization of public life in general because the pragmatics of measuring success (personally and organizationally) displaces the discussion of the whys and wherefores of what is being done. The methodology of measurement (via the computer) and the creation of quantitative "targets" displaces questions about qualitative goals. Rather than being a means, measurement turns into an end in itself.

The implications of the process of rationalization and integration for social control, that is, for "friendly fascism," are not difficult to draw. Within the modern democratic state there exist, increasingly, two "nations" (by no means a new idea): Those who are integrated into the upper levels of the mode of production, participants in the political system and the culture, and those who are, at best, less so and at the extreme constitute the outsiders: the growing number of working poor, the un- and underemployed, the "under-class," the "lumpenproletariat," all of which categories are dispro-portionally members of "racial" minority groups, including large numbers of recent immigrants. Under specific historical conditions (the late 1960s and early 1970s) university students also become dis-affected in very large numbers. In economic terms, there are those who work at the upper levels of technology and services, and for the state, and those who work at the lower levels of secondary services such as office cleaning or food retailing, or in "sweatshop" type industries. The middle, the formerly stable, unionized industrial working class and other middle-stratum income earners, is in decline. And many students begin to realize that the roles promised to them in a time of prosperity are now problematic.

The mix of how this "outsider" element is treated varies from time to time (depending partly on the need for low-paid labor, which is often the key to immigration policy), and from country to country (depending on the strength of oppositional social movements, and the general ideology of the country as it has been shaped by history and culture). But despite such differences, as crime (and occasional terrorist acts) impinges on the public consciousness (propelled in part by the media) the demand for more prisons, longer sentences, executions, and the expulsion of foreigners increases, and the defense of democratic rights weakens. Moreover, the existence of nuclear power and biological weaponry creates a rationale for total, if unattainable, social control as a means of avoiding nuclear theft, terrorism, and catastrophe.

To what extent can we say that Western countries approach the "friendly fascism" definition? In this respect, the United States is far less developed than, say, Germany. What is often termed "political repression" in the United States is still more often a result of con-servative tradition at the local level than a conscious plan on the part of national authorities to inhibit protest in a modern, rational way, although there have been a number of notorious exceptions. Both traditional and modern rational repression forms coexist and overlap. Still, there is a big historical and analytical difference between a lynch mob, or the hysteria of a McCarthy period, and a behavior-modification system in a modern, clean, supposedly well-kept federal prison such as the one in Marion, Illinois, where sensory deprivation and other psychological methods are used to "neutralize" political deviants. It is the latter that is the "model" for "friendly fascism," not gangs of uniformed thugs bashing gays or peaceniks in the street.

Law enforcement in the United States, for reasons both of size and political tradition, is still relatively decentralized, though clearly less so than before World War II. With the advent of such innovations as the FBI Uniform Crime Reports, its computerized criminal history file (only since 1971) and other statistical reporting systems, centralization is clearly on the way, though the United States lags far behind Western European countries, with their more centralized traditions of government. There is not yet, in the United States, an effective domestic passport system; travel is virtually uncontrolled except at the international level, and it is possible for persons to exist underground for a decade or more. Both economy and geography provide interstices where people can make a living (quite apart from organized crime). Finally, the American rhetoric and tradition of individual rights itself acts as a brake on state interference, for better or (in the case of the persistence of ultra-right-wing militia organizations) worse. Nevertheless, a host of executive and legislative measures (frequently introduced by "liberals") have, over the years, moved the country many steps in the direction of a stronger, more repressive state. Measures restricting access to hearings by immigrants, and various pieces of "antiterrorist" legislation are only the most recent in a long series of limitations on individual rights. Generally, measures initiated by liberal Democrats such as Sen. Edward Kennedy (or, formerly, Sen. Hubert Humphrey), and those supported by some Eastern "Establishment" foundations, are oriented to a rational form of social control closer to Gross's idea of friendly fascism, than are the more hysterical measures introduced by right-wing Republicans. The latter are often defeated sooner or later. It is the more carefully conceived "liberal" security measures that persist.

The 1970s can be characterized as the formative period of the modern national security state, insofar as it has developed in Western countries. Although the reasons for this development are complex, it is clear that the growth of social protest movements in the 1960s and 1970s was a major factor, or was at least the major official rationale. No state stands idly by as movements claiming to be, or perceived to be, revolutionary, take the stage. It is therefore worthwhile having a closer look at this formative period, especially in countries of the "welfare state" variety.

Neighboring Canada is a multiparty, stable democracy with a strong social democratic party and labor and cooperative movement. In this modern state, the War Measures Act, suspending all civil liberties throughout the country, was invoked from October 16, 1970 to April 1971 because two persons had been kidnapped by a tiny terrorist cell in Quebec (one of the victims was killed subsequent to the invocation of the act). At that time the entire Quebec Liberation Front (the FLQ) was estimated to have no more than 175 activists and 3,000 sympathizers. Nevertheless, 13,000 troops and police were mobilized to occupy strategic locations in the province. More than 600 people (mainly peace, labor, and community activists) were arrested. (A number of them believed, initially, that they were the victims of a fascist coup!) These were, under the act, subject to being held up to twenty-one days without a charge. There is a similar act in the United Kingdom and in numerous other countries lacking the habeas corpus provisions of U.S. law. The 1970–71 incident broke the back of the FLQ, making it clear that extremism would not be tolerated. Its main leaders were imprisoned. It impelled Quebec nationalists to adopt moderate strategies and programs that today lack any kind of radical economic, much less socialistic content.

Nowhere has "friendly fascism" been developed to the extent it has in the Federal Republic of Germany, where layer upon layer of justifications for security measures unheard of in the United States exist—from the position that Hitler's rise was due to inadequate measures being taken against extremism in the Weimar Republic, to the dangers the student movement posed to civilized university and public life in the 1970s, to (formerly) East German spying and agitation, to the realities of international terrorism, to the rise of neo-Nazism and even the alleged threat of the Scientology Church. While it is only fair to say that there has been a grain of truth behind each justification, it is equally fair to say that there was much more to the rise of Hitler than inadequate legal measures. Entirely adequate measures existed on the books as they do in every society; they simply were not put into force. Moreover, although the immense legal apparatus erected in Germany to cope with the dangers of extremism and terror ultimately put an end to "left-wing" underground activity, it did so at the expense of eliminating many protections of the civil liberties of ordinary citizens. The cost in inhibiting legitimate, legal oppositional elements by encouraging a "purge" atmosphere throughout the society was, and continues to be, considerable. Furthermore, these measures did not inhibit the growth of the extremist Right. Only now that a huge public outcry has forced political leaders to mobilize the police against neo-Nazi terror, has the traditional "blindness in the right eye" of the authorities begun to come to an end.

In the decade ending January 1977, the formative period of Germany's national security state, twenty-eight people were killed by domestic terrorists (excluding the Munich Olympics tragedy). In turn, fifteen terrorists were killed by police in shootouts, plus other deaths in prison. These terrorist acts on the part of the Red Army Fraction and other small underground grouplets that formed the tiny army of the frustrated extreme Left (somewhat parallel to the Weather Underground in the United States) became the justification for an unprecedented (since the Third Reich) expansion of domestic police forces. Between 1969 and 1971 the Bundeskriminalamt (BKA, similar to the FBI) more than doubled its budget. The Bundesgrenz-schutz (formerly the Border Guard, now a nationwide tactical police unit used in most demonstrations, with armed personnel carriers, heavy weapons, helicopters, etc.) went from 16,700 officers in 1969 to 22,159 in 1973; the Verfassungsschutz (Office for the Protection of the Constitution, the political police) doubled its budget in four years. By 1975 an electronic data processing system, INPOL, had been completed for internal use; it contained information on 231,000 persons. A similar process was underway in Norway, where there was virtually no terrorist activity in those years. In the decade 1966–1977 police expenditures nearly quintupled.

Some observers believe that the West German response to the perceived threat of terrorism and extremism by way of an expansion of the police apparatus was based on the U.S. model, where local police forces beefed up their personnel and armament in the period of urban riots and antiwar mobilizations from 1964 through 1972. But Germany went far beyond mere expansion of the police. Following the "friendly fascism" model, the West German state enlarged its security measures in three other areas: (1) A plethora of provisions in the criminal code effectively criminalizing some forms of criticism of the established order and its public servants; censoring books, posters, and the press; and subjecting writers, distributors, printers, editors, and dealers to fine and imprisonment if they are involved with works deemed by police or judges as conducive to "violence"; as well as provisions broadening the authority of police to "stop and frisk," set up street controls, raid apartment houses, etc.; (2) new legal provisions insolating accused and convicted prisoners from contact with legal counsel and indeed from the entire outside world under given conditions, and seriously infringing on confidentiality rights between prisoners and counsel, as well as enabling courts to disbar lawyers or prevent them from defending specific accused persons; and (3) administrative enactments under the civil service code subjecting all civil servants and applicants for public sector jobs to loyalty-security screenings. These rules prevent the hiring and require the termination, regardless of tenure (which in Germany extends to many state employees), of anyone concerning whom "doubt" exists that he or she is, or in the future will be, able to "stand up actively and at all times for the free and democratic foundations of the society." Such doubt can be and has been based on a wide variety of perfectly legal political activities and utterances ranging from running for public office on a Communist ticket to writing letters to the newspaper protesting the firing of someone else under these provisions.

In the Federal Republic of Germany there was then no hint of any economic dislocation on the horizon to justify Establishment concern about widespread unrest. Nevertheless there were raids on bookstores and publishing houses; fines and prison sentences for writers and editors; large-scale street "stops and frisks" involving, on occasion, tens of thousands of vehicles on their way to a demonstration opposing a nuclear power facility; firings and nonhirings of thousands of individuals who are politically suspect but stand unconvicted of any crime; and the occasional use of quasi-torture methods in prisons (mainly in the form of total isolation, but also acoustical deprivation [keeping people in soundproof cells], the manipulation of lighting, and beatings).

In the Germany of today, security measures including the use of the Border Guard to patrol public-transportation sites such as railway stations and subway platforms and to stop, check papers, and frisk persons randomly, are justified by politicians of all major parties as a way of tracking down illegal immigrants and deterring street crime (including skinhead violence). Representatives of the homeless and other poor people, however, insist that increased policing is aimed at "cleansing" areas of the city of "undesirable" elements, thereby making center-city areas more palatable to tourists, real-estate interests, and middle-class people more generally. In 1998 the somewhat restrictive rules under which police were already tapping more than 6,000 phones per year were broadened. The constitutional protection of the sanctity of the home was formally amended to permit authorities virtually unrestricted bugging of homes, with the rationale that this was required to monitor criminal racketeering. Professionals such as doctors, lawyers, and midwives were exempted.

In examining any single state, no one phenomenon alone justifies the prognosis that the state is becoming a "national security" or "friendly fascist" state. Moreover, even with a pattern of symptoms, there is no modern state that is the "perfect" or "ideal-typical" model. Each state is somewhere on a range within this typology, with Germany perhaps farther toward the type envisioned by Lasswell or Gross than others. What are the indices of the trend toward such a type?

1. The gradual encroachment of the state into areas formerly operated by private, voluntary, alternative institutions, what is often called "civil society," so that state expertise comes to supplant spontaneous efforts to participate in public life. In the Federal Republic of Germany state authorities have veto power over professorial hiring, often determine the structure and mission of museums, demand that librarians supply the names of borrowers of leftist books, etc. Yet this development is in the process of being reversed in the United States where many state-supported cultural enterprises are being forcibly privatized in the name of budgetary restraint. And there is pressure to do the same in other Western countries.

2. A nationally coordinated welfare structure guaranteeing a minimum income or some form of job in a context of planning, a social "net" widely supported by labor unions and social democratic parties, and at one time even by the United States Democratic Party. Yet this strategy, presumably undertaken as a cooptative reform move in order to undermine more radical solutions, is also being reversed in the U.S., and efforts in this direction in Western Europe are presently stalled only because of mass-protest demonstrations against cutbacks.

3. A gradual merger of welfare and criminal justice apparatuses so that they are no longer easily distinguishable: police do social work, social workers identify potential criminals, teachers flag potential future deviants. The two sets of behaviors become less dis-

tinguishable by criminalizing deviant acts, and by medicalizing and psychiatrizing criminal acts. This merger necessitates an information-exchange system in which an individual's record in one area (e.g., health) becomes accessible to all other institutional areas (an arrest for drunken driving in Sweden is reported to a welfare agency; the U.S. court system offers an army enlistment as an alternative to prison; the army becomes a career or vocational trainer). As the head of the German BKA put it some years ago, "The police must change itself into an agency for social change, into an organ for advising and consulting on politics and legislation.... [It] possesses a unique access to insights...concerning the structural defects of society... [thus] a system could be created that would anticipate problems *before* they arise."[16]

4. The cross-national coordination of police forces, including information exchange, training, and special assistance on projects, including even command of one nation's personnel by officers from another nation: In short, the internationalization of police systems, under the rubric of the "war on terrorism," the "war on drugs," etc.

5. An internal passport and registration system so that all changes in residence and virtually all travel is susceptible to checks.

6. Necessarily, as a concomitant of several of the above, an international centralized electronic data-processing information bank on all residents of the countries involved.

7. The elaboration of legal measures covering "crimes" that are at least in part political in nature, such as the new "antiterrorism" legislation of the United States (but such measures have been in place in other countries for many years). This legislation includes provisions for extradition, so that, for example, alleged Irish Republican Army, or Palestinian, terrorists can be extradited from the United States to the United Kingdom, or to Israel, with little or nothing in the way of hearings.

8. The integration of national public and private policy-forming and advisory bodies with those of other nations. The best example is the Trilateral Commission, which has generated study

groups on, among other subjects, the alleged dangers of an excess of democracy.

However, as a country begins to approach "friendly fascism," it confronts certain contradictions that inhibit its full development. The clearest and most current contradiction is the decline of the credibility of the social democratic or reformist state that theoretically was supposed to combine economic with political (internal) security. The rise of "Thatcherism" or "Reaganism" represents the triumph of a thesis claiming that the welfare state has become ungovernable because it is too expensive, hence inhibits economic prosperity. The line of reasoning is quite interesting: state intervention in the economy comes about because laissez-faire business is inherently unstable, leading to crises and social disruption. The state then becomes identified with economic success (by the politicians who run it), but then also with failure as the economy begins to stumble. The state then becomes the scapegoat for failed policies, whether or not of its own making. This "narrative" is able to account for a variety of dysfunctional events ranging from unemployment to crime to the growth of the welfare rolls, offering an instant solution to many different parts of society, a solution that boils down to shrinking the public sector.[17] The contradiction resides in the fact that giving more rein to private enterprise (by deregulating, for instance) means returning to the chaos of a less-regulated economy, one in which cooptative welfare measures have been cut back, thus leading anew to crisis and social disruption. In any event, the success of the ungovernability (or as it is sometimes called, the "overload") thesis means that the march toward a total integration or *Gleichschaltung* of the society is slowed or halted altogether.

A deeper contradiction, of which the above "narrative" is subsidiary, has to do with what is called the legitimation crisis.[18] As Alan Wolfe has argued, "Any ruling class must seek more than the maximization of its privileges; it must seek to legitimate itself as well."[19] The state must take some measures to maintain some degree of popularity, especially in a society in which political participation has been won through hard struggle. Such a struggle changes "the dynamics by which politics takes place": democracy becomes part of the legitimate way of conducting political business (including the arrangement of a policy consensus among the various fractions of the ruling class and their allies). This requires the maintenance of democratic forms and acts as a check on repression. However, as Claus Offe has pointed out, "by supporting capitalist commodity production, it cannot but support those forces of accumulation that result in... the irreversible 'dropping out' of growing parts of both labor and capital."[20] More, and larger, fractions of classes within the mode of production become disaffected as they become disadvantaged by the capitalist dynamic. As this disaffection takes political form, as people come to insist that their lives "should no longer be controlled by capitalist 'market forces,'" the efficient operation of capital becomes impeded, forcing the capitalist state to repress popular forces, hence delegitimating itself. There is, then, a fundamental contradiction between capitalist efficiency in the interest of accumulation, and capitalist legitimacy. This contradiction is suppressed in "Third World" states because crisis is more endemic, and because bourgeois fractions that have an interest in legitimacy (perhaps for reasons of international public relations) are too weak.

The accumulation agenda today takes place in the context of a growing global marketplace, what is sometimes called "globalization." In this context, as Ellen Meiksins Wood has argued, "capital needs the state to maintain the conditions of accumulation, to preserve labor discipline, to enhance the mobility of capital.... U.S. capital, in its quest for 'competitiveness,' demands a state that will keep social costs to a minimum, while keeping in check the social conflict and disorder generated by the absence of social provision."[21] The nation-state will also, she believes, "continue to play a central role as capital's channel into the global market." These are not easy tasks to juggle.

The contradiction between the accumulation agenda (the drive toward profit and growth within capitalism) and the legitimation agenda (the need for popular acceptance of capitalism in the interest of stabilty) has generated a limited level of crisis, even though that crisis is not (yet?) of major proportions. The accumultion agenda has led to increasing inequality of income and wealth within, and between, nations, as Jerry Kloby, among others, has amply documented.[22] Income and wealth inequality in the United States are the worst in the "First World." Although official U.S. unemployment rates are one-third those of Western Europe, where they have been running an average of 13 to 15 percent in recent years, a good deal of job growth is at the lower services sector end: janitors, salespersons, guards, home health aides, etc. Moreover, U.S. rates are kept artificially low in part because the "employed" armed forces are counted "in" the labor force, while the imprisoned "unemployed" (in a country with the highest incarceration rate of the "Western" world) are not. About 10 percent of U.S. job growth is in the contingent (temps, etc.) field. Close to 40 million Americans, including nearly one child out of every five, live under the official poverty line. Meanwhile, the best-off 1 percent of households controls more net worth than the bottom 90 percent, the highest concentration of wealth since 1929.

The crisis aspect is that such growing inequality makes for more conflict between class, racial, gender, and other groups within the society; in short, it leads to disruptions that are damaging to the orderliness, the discipline required to operate a modern economy. As the post–World War II economic miracle began to tarnish in the mid-1970s, with shrinking profit margins and rising unemployment rates in many countries, capitalist states began to face a choice of which side of the contradiction between accumulation and legitimation to favor. The pressure to increase profit necessarily leads to fiscal and political measures (including the reining in of organized labor) that squeeze workers. As protest mounts, political repression often follows. If on the other hand legitimation remains a priority, expensive reforms (generous unemployment and retirement payments, health benefits, increases in real wages) will be sustained or increased. Legitimation also implies political participation, the opposite of repression. The more participation in the political process, the more mobilization in the streets, the more pressure for still more benefits. But such gains endanger accumulation, forcing a reassessment of agendas. The argument that high unemployment is traceable to overly generous benefits rather than to the availability of decent-paying jobs, gains force, and unemployment and other components of the social "net" are shredded, to the advantage of the accumulation agenda. Capitalism becomes less kind, less gentle. Homelessness, and hunger, grow, and private charities are asked to fill the gap (the more they do so, the stronger the argument that state provisions are unnecessary, the more they must do, etc.). Repression increases as those employed in the criminal countereconomy are shunted off to prison for every minor crime (in the United States this means particularly nonviolent drug offenses).

As the proportion of resources going into social control increases, the delivery of services deteriorates further. Client populations become more restive. Yet if concessions were to be provided, breathing space for social movements of protest would be possible. So, which is it to be, repression in the interest of accumulation, as in most Third World national security states, or reform in the interest of social peace? The "friendly fascism" model implies that these agendas can coexist, as to some extent they do. But this is not a peaceful coexistence because large-scale interests are at stake. The fractions of capital are rarely unified about how these agendas, which compete for resources and are therefore always in tension, are to be combined.

The various fractions of capital, elements of the state bureaucracy, and even segments of the leadership of the labor movement, while agreeing that the system must be made to survive, differ on how this is to be done, specifically, what proportion of state resources should go to welfare and other increases in real income, versus areas that directly aid the process of capital accumulation (government expenditure on hardware, business-oriented R&D (research and development), foreign aid of certain kinds, internal security measures, and even measures dampening the strength of labor). These debates theoretically create a space in which political discourse can continue in a more or less open way, both inside the parties and in a wider public arena, since so long as there is no unanimity concerning strategy, so long as the fractions of capital and their allies argue, will the rest of the population be left relatively at peace.

But this relative peace is itself a strategy. As was pointed out in the previous chapter, democratic structures in the "Third World" can be and often are covers for behind-the-scenes oligarchic rule. Although free-market economics may be accompanied by free-market politics, too much democracy is dangerous, as the elite group known as the Trilateral Commission pointed out in several studies in the 1970s.[23] "Free-market democracy" needs to be promoted to dampen mass insurgency, but contained so that stable government can be assured. "Low-intensity" democracy can thus be "used to obtain the consent of the governed while excluding more 'excessive' or high intensity forms of democracy."[24] The object is to "use polyarchic [pluralistic] institutions in preference to more authoritarian forms of government in order to 'produce more social control with less coercive pressure.'" Although this approach was mainly intended for application in the Third World, this is clearly consistent with the "friendly fascism" framework.

The national security state in its developing "friendly" form will be with us for some time (that is, short of its "model" or final form as envisaged by the pessimists of both Right and Left). Contradictions will continue to exist, leaving room for noninstitutionally integrated locii of political and economic power. Given the assumption that some form of parliamentary democracy must be permitted in order to provide an arena in which to attain a functioning consensus among the fractions of the ruling class, as well as providing a sense that the state is legitimate for most of the populace, it will be possible to protest excessive security measures. The very rhetoric of "human rights" is a weapon in their protection, and at least a partial shield against repression.

The friendly fascism model provides us with some conceptual

tools with which to analyze trends in the development of the modern state. It affords us a set of warning signs that we ignore at our peril. But the total ideological, cultural, political, and economic hegemony of the ruling class that is implied, and sometimes explicitly claimed, in this model is not yet here.

# NOTES

1. Bertram Gross, *Friendly Fascism* (Boston: South End Press, 1980).

2. Friedrich Hayek, *The Road to Serfdom* (Chicago: University of Chicago Press, 1944).

3. James Burnham, *The Managerial Revolution* (New York: John Day, 1941).

4. Herbert Marcuse, *One-Dimensional Man* (Boston: Beacon Press, 1964).

5. Max Horkheimer and Theodor W. Adorno, *Dialectic of Enlightenment* (New York: Seabury Press, 1972).

6. Daniel Bell, *The End of Ideology* (Glencoe, Ill.: Free Press, 1960).

7. Ralph Miliband, *The State in Capitalist Society* (New York: Basic-Books, 1969), 268.

8. Harold Lasswell, "The Garrison State," *American Journal of Sociology* 46 (January 1941): 455–68.

9. Horkheimer and Adorno, *Dialectic of Enlightenment*, 35–36.

10. Marcuse, *One-Dimensional Man*, 3.

11. Brad Rose, "The Triumph of Social Control? A Look at Herbert Marcuse's *One-Dimensional Man*, Twenty-Five Years Later," *Berkeley Journal of Sociology* 35 (1990): 61.

12. Alan Wolfe, *The Seamy Side of Democracy* (New York: David McKay, 1973), 21.

13. Ibid., 209.

14. H. H. Gerth and C. Wright Mills, eds., *From Max Weber: Essays in Sociology* (New York: Oxford University Press, 1946), chap. 8.

15. James O'Connor, *The Fiscal Crisis of the State* (New York: St. Martin's Press, 1973).

16. *Die Polizei* (Zentralorgan fuer das Sicherheits- und Ordnungswesen Polizei-Wissenschaft-Recht-Praxis), May 1972.

17. Colin Hay, *Re-Stating Social and Political Change* (Buckingham, United Kingdom: Open University Press, 1996), chap. 5.

18. For more extensive discussions of this concept see: Juergen Habermas, *Legitimation Crisis* (London: Heinemann, 1975); Hay, *Re-Stating Social and Political Change*, 88–98; Bob Jessup, *The Capitalist State* (New York: New York University Press, 1982), 106–12; Claus Offe, "The Theory of the Capitalist State and the Problem of Policy Formation," in Leon Lindberg et al., *Stress and Contradiction in Modern Capitalism* (Lexington, Mass.: Lexington Books, 1975); and Alan Wolfe, *The Limits of Legitimacy* (New York: Free Press, 1977), esp. chap. 10.

19. Wolfe, *The Seamy Side of Democracy*, xiii ff.

20. Offe, in Lindberg, 245 ff.

21. Ellen Meiksins Wood, "Labor, the State, and Class Struggle," *Monthly Review* (July–August 1997): 12.

22. Jerry Kloby, *Inequality, Power, and Development* (Amherst, N.Y.: Humanity Books, 1997), chaps. 3, 7. Also see *Left Business Observer* no. 71 (January 22, 1996), which reports on the findings of the Luxembourg Income Study. There are many other sources for this general finding.

23. Michel Crozier, Samuel P. Huntington, and Joji Watanuki, *The Crisis of Democracy* (New York: New York University Press, 1975).

24. John Bellamy Foster, review of *Promoting Polyarchy*, by William I. Robinson, in *Monthly Review* (September 1997): 54–55. Quotes are from Crozier, "Western Europe," in *The Crisis of Democracy*.

# 4

# CORPORATE CAPITAL AND STATE POLICY

*What the president of the United States is thinking about is, more often than not, precisely what the big corporate people are thinking about, often in the same terms: war or peace, balance of international payments, treaties, unemployment and wages, gross national product, interest rates, consumer finance, national debt, taxes, etc. etc.*

—Ferdinand Lundberg[1]

*Segments of the economic elite have violated democratic political and legal processes, with differing degrees of effort and success in the various periods of American history, but in no recent period could they correctly be said to have controlled the elected and appointed political authorities in large measure.*

—Arnold M. Rose[2]

These two quotations, the first by a once well-known muckraker, the other by a respected academic sociologist, represent in summary form the two basic, conflicting theories of the relationship between economic elites and the state in Western society. There are numerous subdivisions and controversies within each of these broad schools of thought, but ultimately they are of secondary importance, dealing more with methods of inquiry, and with measures of degree than with the substance of the issue.

Of course methods of inquiry are closely related to theory in that theorists do choose those methods that tend to produce results supporting their theories, so that the notion of an "objective" or truly neutral scientific methodology in social science, especially in a value-laden and controversial area like power structures, is an illusion. Nevertheless, some theories are, on balance, more persuasive than others even if they cannot be "proven" beyond any reasonable doubt. And although the issue of the degree to which a particular approach is true, which really means the degree to which a theory, though generally right, needs to be qualified, is secondary does not mean it is unimportant because accurate understandings of complexities are essential, especially for those who want to intervene in historical events. Bad theory, or even good overall theory that is sloppy in the details, leads to bad political strategy.

The first view quoted above is shorthand for the idea that the state carries out its domestic and international policies on behalf, if not necessarily "at the behest" or direct orders of, economic elites (specifically, the ruling capitalist class).[3] The state is not neutral; rather its very structure, its constitution, its legal framework, reflects the interests of the ruling class (even if not perfectly, and even if modified by the need to provide concessions to other classes in order to ensure stability). The second perspective, which is often linked to "pluralist" theory, says that the state is more or less neutral, an empty building into which policy content is poured as the end result of the interaction of many interest groups, including big business, and that even business lacks the kind of internal consensus that would make it much more than the senior partner in the democratic enterprise. A variation of this second approach is that in the contemporary world states themselves constitute "potent and autonomous organizational actors."[4] The point of view of this book is that the weight of the evidence generally supports the first approach, despite necessary qualifications and despite complexities that might make Lundberg's bald statement sound somewhat extreme to careful observers.

The capitalist class is a ruling class. As a ruling class, it does its utmost to exercise its power to make decisions according to its interests. Regardless of all sorts of exceptions and qualifications, modifications and concessions under specific historic circumstances, "in capitalist society the state (is) above all the coercive instrument of a ruling class, itself defined in terms of its ownership and control of the means of production," or, as the *Communist Manifesto* put it, it is "but a committee for managing the common affairs of the whole bourgeoisie."[5] This is in fact consistent with Lundberg's quotation. Note that he does not say that the president (of the United States) takes orders from "big corporate people" in the sense that telephone calls from Wall Street to the White House are how policy is conducted. What he says is that the president and "big corporate people" *think about the same things, in the same way.* What this means is that the president, who is the head of the state, and major corporation leaders, the heads of the economy, come from the same general social milieu, and even if they don't (some presidents clearly had social origins different from those of the Eastern elite) that they have been socialized into the same values, the same appreciations of what needs to be done to assure the survival of the system, so that phone calls are not even necessary. Even more, it implies that the president, or if not the president him- or herself, but certainly many state officials, and corporate leaders, *are the same people*, forming an interacting elite in which individuals simply exchange their business hats for political hats from time to time when convenient or necessary. This is a very important idea, one that will be explored in some detail later in this chapter.

Pluralist theory denies all of this and claims, moreover, that empirical evidence will not support the notion that economic elites control governments in democratic societies. This idea, pluralists say, is a holdover from days when business was more powerful, and when populists of both Left and Right promoted "Wall Street conspiracy" theories in order to gain political advantage. The era of trust-busting, of regulation of business, what is known in American history as the Progressive Era (roughly 1890 to 1920, but also Roosevelt's New Deal), effectively reined Big Business in, and led to a state that was, if not free of business intervention, surely not controlled or dominated by capital.[6]

The pluralist model therefore argues that political power is much more diffused than can be accounted for by "elite" theory.[7] In a famous study of New Haven, Connecticut, political scientist Robert Dahl, for example, argued that the competition of voluntary associations or interest groups, and the existence of competing political parties that also involve large numbers of people, insure that a marketplace of differing views will exist, and the power of wealth will be contained. Social policy is therefore the outcome of the interactions and the bargaining that takes place among many groups, representing many people. As such, policy represents a moderate social consensus, since extreme views will be overwhelmed and ultimately outvoted by coalitions that will want to prevent any one group from accumulating too much power. When "big business" gets too powerful, therefore, regulatory legislation follows; when "big labor" gets too pushy, we get legislation limiting the power of labor. In this picture, "all the active and legitimate groups in the population can make themselves heard at some crucial point in the process of decision," as Dahl put it.[8] This does not mean there are no elites. In some versions of the theory there are numerous elites, but each elite dominates only one sphere of power, and there is no overall cohesion among them. Indeed, the competition between elites "is itself a prime guarantee that power in society *will* be diffused, and not concentrated," as Miliband (who profoundly disagrees with this approach) summarizes it.[9] The state's policies, then, embody the outcome of this widely dispersed system of competition. It represents the consensus that develops out of the participation of all active groups, both elite and nonelite.

Elite and other theorists of various stripes have leveled numerous criticisms at the pluralist approach. Dahl's work in particular has come under scrutiny because it appears to contradict many other community studies over the years, the vast majority finding that relatively small numbers of economic and social leaders dominate most important community-level decisions. One area of criticism has to do with the kind of decisions that are being studied: elites may, and do, fail to intervene in issues that are not particularly relevant to them, thus giving the impression that other groups have more power than they really do. These are called "nondecisions": the decision not to intervene in a decision, to leave it up to the public, is itself a decision just as important as the decision to intervene. But it leaves the impression that democracy is at work.[10] Moreover, "in the case of political nominations, there is no evidence that it makes any difference" who is nominated or elected, since business leaders have access to mayors regardless of party by virtue of campaign financing, and personal, that is, social, contact.[11] An even more significant criticism, however, is that most people have little if any connection to interest groups, and even when they do, most interest groups (like churches or social clubs) do not involve themselves in politics. Even when they do, their involvement and power is not in proportion to their numbers. That is, some very small organizations have a great deal of influence, while others with millions of members (or hundreds, at the local level) have virtually no input into decisions because they lack the interlocking relationships, the social connections, that are the prerequisite to real decision- or nondecision-making power.[12] In the final analysis, as G. William Domhoff demonstrates in his restudy of Dahl's work, a relatively small number of business leaders who are also members of the social elite dominate the really important decisions even in New Haven. The state in its local variant represents the needs of local capital, which in most cases have to do with property: real estate, development, planning, and infrastructure (roads, highways, public and private transportation). As Domhoff summarizes it, "a community power structure is at bottom an aggregate of land-based interests that profit from increasingly intensive use of land," which expresses itself as population growth. "A successful local elite is one that is able to attract the corporate plants and offices, the defense contracts, the federal and state agencies, or the educational and research establishments that lead to an expanded work force, and then in turn to an expansion of retail and other commercial activity."[13] Hence the agenda of local government is normally to be an instrument of this overall "growth machine," which is synonymous with creating a good business environment: low business taxes, efficient government (including law enforcement) services, and a reliable labor force, just as is the case with national government, and for similar reasons. The dominant focus is ever on the accumulation of capital, profitability, and the survival of the system, blended in with the need for legitimation. It follows that pluralist theory is part of the ideology of legitimation since it claims that there is no community power structure, and that governmental decisions are the result of the interplay of diverse and diffused interest groups.

Assuming, as we do throughout this book, that states reflect the interests of ruling classes, two quite fascinating questions arise: who, exactly, are these people who are the ruling class, and what, exactly, does the ruling class do when it rules?[14] There is a great deal of published material on both these issues. The first question is a fairly common one among those who study power structures. Therborn calls it the subjectivist approach because it looks for the *subject* of power: "A few, many, a unified class of families, an institutional elite of top decision-makers... ," etc. The second is a more structural approach: not who, but how much, and how is it put into practice? What do rulers do when they rule; where do they lead? The first question looks at people; the second, at outcomes. Both are quite important, indeed they are so closely interrelated that it makes little sense to separate them, although empirical studies often do that. They are inseparable because if we are to understand the nature of power structures, we need to know what makes actors do what they do, and we need to know what the relationship is between what makes them do what they do, and what it is that they do. They are of one fabric. People (in general) are not separate from what they do. We assume further, in line with all sociological thought, that people's backgrounds, their social or class standing (which implies their family background, their education or socialization, their various formal and informal memberships) generally have a significant impact on their values, which importantly inform their actions when they arrive in decision-making positions. This idea is basic to power structure research, and deserves closer examination.

Power structure research focusing on the study of elites, who they are and what they do, falls into two opposing political camps. These camps are in substantial agreement that there are ruling groups, but disagree as to their merit. What might be called the "aristocratic" camp is best exemplified by the work of the late E. Digby Baltzell, a University of Pennsylvania sociologist who was himself a participant and an acute observer of the Philadelphia area social and economic establishment. The other camp, which we might characterize as that of the democratic critics of elite society, is represented by figures such as C. Wright Mills, G. William Domhoff, and, in a different way, by the Marxist school.

Baltzell felt that "no nation can long endure without both the liberal democratic and the authoritative aristocratic processes."[15] By "democratic" he meant that the elite should be "open," and talented people from the lower orders able to rise into it. By "aristocracy" he meant that group of upper-class families "born to positions of high prestige...because their ancestors have been leaders (elite members) for one generation or more," a group that supposedly promotes a set of values representing the entire population, and continues to provide leadership of the basic institutions of society. Such an open aristocracy, he thought, would assure stability and act as guardians of enlightened civilization, but only if artificial barriers to leadership such as racial and religious discrimination were removed. It is a view that goes back to Plato's *Repubic*, and his argument that society should be ruled by philosopher-kings.

Baltzell's primary subject of study was "the Philadelphia gentlemen," those upper-class males who could be identified by their listing in *The Social Register*, and also their presence in *Who's Who in America*. What is significant in Baltzell's observation is that "the higher the functional position, the more important social connections or social class considerations become."[16] In short, class connections lead to elite positions, and over several generations, elite positions lead to membership in the aristocratic upper class, what is normally called "society." Baltzell's research tells us who is in charge, and a good deal about their values. The significance of this link between elite status and aristocracy has to do with cohesion or consensus when it comes to policy, "because those who own and control the major concentrations of national wealth encounter each other in a private sphere of informal relations."[17] These informal relations begin with attendance at exclusive prep schools, continue through student life at elite private universities, and are later buttressed by membership in certain top men's social clubs. This artistocracy also has high rates of intermarriage, membership in traditionally upper-class churches (particularly the Episcopalian), and tends to cluster in, obviously, high-priced and exclusive residential areas, so that the interaction that is the basis of shared values is ongoing. There are occasional mavericks, of course, but it flies in the face of sociological reason to pretend that such a group, whether at the local or national level, lacks a cohesive, *general* outlook. It is this outlook that inevitably has a profound impact on state policy when that policy is formed and carried out by members of this same group. Baltzell, however, was not particularly interested in the relationship between the upper class and the state. Aside from an extensive discussion of the "schizophrenia" with which business elements regarded Franklin D. Roosevelt in his *The Protestant Establishment*, Baltzell's work is more in the nature of cultural history, the culture or patterns of daily behavior of the upper class.

Given the rootedness of this upper class in the ownership of wealth going back several generations, something that Baltzell takes as a matter of course, it would be naive to assume that the protection of capital and the survival of the capitalist system that is the basis of their wealth is irrelevant or secondary to state policy. When we turn to an examination of specific state policies at both the domestic and international levels the evidence that the state (via its leading personnel, who are often members of both social and economic elites, as well as being state officials) promotes the general interest of the upper class is overwhelming. But most of this research has been done by the democratic critics of elites, not by those who view elites as positive contributors to society.

The precise way this works is subject to a considerable amount of debate, however. One of the pioneers in examining the way the "power elite" works was C. Wright Mills, in his famous book of that title. He defined the power elite as "those political, economic, and military circles which as an intricate set of overlapping cliques share decisions having at least national consequences."[18] Two aspects of his approach are particularly important: first, that there are *three* elite-dominated areas (somewhat like the three overlapping rings in the familiar beer logo); and second, that at their apex, or in the overlapping core of the three rings, "the leading men in each of the three domains of power—the warlords, the corporation chieftains, the political directorate—tend to come together, to form the power elite of America."[19] His key idea is that of the interlock among these separate elites, their interdependence. Mills also sees the people of these "higher circles" as members of an "inner circle" that constitutes a "more or less compact social and psychological entity,"[20] that is, they share a common outlook, an idea that is not inconsistent with Baltzell's approach at all.

However, Mills does not share Baltzell's view that these higher circles represent a positive force in society. To the contrary, he felt strongly that "in the name of realism its men of decision enforce their often crackpot definitions upon world reality..." by which he was referring primarily to the nuclear arms race and the cold war of the time. The elite is potent, and makes conscious decisions that are overwhelmingly negative in their consequences for humanity, Mills thought. In his later book, *The Causes of World War III*, he specifically indicts both Soviet and American elites as being unrepresentative of their populations, and for putting the world at risk.[21]

In the view of Marxists such as Paul Sweezy, Mills overestimated the power of the military and politicians as quasi-independent forces.[22] Both groups, Sweezy felt, are dependent upon the capitalist class that rules the economic institutions, the people Mills called "the corporate rich." Yet the research conducted by some of Mills's followers suggests that identifying an individual as a member of one or another elite (and thereby weighing the importance of that elite in a particular decision) is really not the point. Even when the political elite (say, in the form of the Department of State) determines a specific policy, it almost always does so consistent with the corporate sector's definition of U.S. interests, a definition that is deeply entrenched in the thinking of all leading members of the political and military establishments, regardless of which party is in the White House or controls Congress. This thinking is based partly on the enculturation of that group, partly on the influence of corporate-sponsored policy groups, and (perhaps most important) on the empirical fact that the definition of a particular individual as a member of "the government," "the military," or "the corporate sector" is an artificial one because of the exchange and overlap of personnel between these worlds. The fact that Allen W. Dulles, to cite but one example, happened to head the CIA at a particular moment in time did not make him a member of the "political elite" rather than some other elite. He was a member of the upper circle of the ruling class, so that his particular position at any given time was irrelevant.[23]

There is a great deal of evidence about this circulation of members of the upper class, and about their interaction socially. Here we are concerned primarily with the interpenetration or permeability of the corporate with the state sector, however, on the assumption that it is the former that primarily influences the latter. What that means is that state policy is not independent or autonomous as a general rule, a point of some controversy among the critics of elite society in recent years.

Critical elite theory claiming that the corporate sector utilizes the state to promote its own interests at least in general if not in every particular is often referred to as "instrumentalism": the state is an instrument of the ruling class. This group of theorists ranges from some classical Marxists like Miliband to power-elite theorists like C. Wright Mills, and in more recent years power-structure researchers like Domhoff and a long list of those who in varying degrees follow in their tradition or use their work as a takeoff point.[24] The research undertaken by this loose grouping has provided ample evidence about interlocks. What it has not done is to account sufficiently for events in which the ruling class has apparently not held sway, or where the coherence that elite theory assumes has not been present. The effect of mass movements on elite policy, which has been referred to as the "legitimation" issue, has also been largely ignored.

How is it possible for individual members of the upper class to change their fields (from corporate law firms to the Department of Defense, for instance), given that the expertise required is presumably somewhat different? Jerry Kloby puts it concisely: "These individuals occupy the positions they do not because of their expertise, but because they embody the interests of their class. By filling important positions in government... with... emissaries of the upper class, the upper class is able to ensure that its wishes will be expressed and that the system will continue to shower its members with a disproportionate amount of the nation's wealth, along with elevated status and power."[25]

An interesting case study involves an interlock between the corporate sector, think tanks, a major university, and the U.S. government. By 1948, as Domhoff describes it, the cold war had become a logical strategy flowing from an assumption that made "American economic prosperity coterminous with global hegemony outside the Soviet Union and Eastern Europe."[26] The Carnegie Corporation, a philanthropic foundation set up by Andrew Carnegie many years before, decided to fund the Harvard Russian Research Center that year, in line with that assumption. In the Summer of 1948, a famous American sociologist, Talcott Parsons, was dispatched to Germany by the director of this new center, Clyde Kluckhohn, an equally well-known anthropologist, in order to identify sources of information (or intelligence) on the Soviet Union, and facilitate bringing some of these individuals to the United States. These sources were Soviet emigrés living in West Germany. Some were wanted as war criminals and Nazi collaborators. The research that Kluckhohn, Parsons, and their Harvard scholarly colleagues was undertaking was funded largely by air force intelligence. The Russian Research Center had close liaison with the State Department and the CIA. The plan to utilize the Russian emigrés was approved by Undersecretary of State Robert Lovett, who had many Wall Street connections, and who would become secretary of defense, and later return to Wall Street as a banker.

So the Carnegie Corporation promoted a think tank at Harvard, named the personnel who would run it, and determined its overall research priorities. The center's research was funded by intelligence agencies and followed an agenda set by the U.S. Air Force. This agenda was fully supported by sociologist Parsons and anthropologist Kluckhohn, and backed by Harvard which, of course, benefited financially and in terms of its social connections from this arrangement.[27] The Carnegie official promoting the creation of the Harvard Russian Research Center, John W. Gardner, was to become President Johnson's Secretary of Health, Education and Welfare, and later on became a director of New York Telephone, Shell Oil, and American Airlines, among other corporations.

Other ventures funded by the Carnegie Corporation included the Council on Foreign Relations, perhaps the most important nongovernmental organization influencing U.S. foreign policy then and now. Carnegie's board of trustees, which was heavily weighted toward Wall Street corporations, overlapped membership with the council. Carnegie and the council also had links to Harvard's board of overseers. Allen W. Dulles, a member of a prominent Wall Street law firm and later head of the CIA, was president of the council at this time.

This fascinating case illustrates Domhoff's analysis of the "policy-planning network" of foundations, think tanks, specialized research institutes, and policy-discussion groups that constitute "the programmatic political party for the upper class and the corporate community, a major element in the power elite."[28] The outcome, in this case Parsons's trip to Germany, was the result of a complex flow of influences and money, from the corporate rich and their corporations to foundations like Carnegie and universities like Harvard, to policy-planning groups such as the Council on Foreign Relations, to research "think tanks" such as the Russian Research Center, which in turn was fed agendas by elements of the executive branch of the U.S. government which were, themselves, manned by people with close connections to the corporate world. Many of the people involved in these decisions shared memberships in elite social clubs. In this particular case, nearly all of Carnegie's trustees, as well as the large majority of Council on Foreign Policy directors, belonged to one or more of these clubs in New York or Washington, the most relevant in terms of interlocks being the Century Association of New York, and the Metropolitan and Cosmos Clubs in Washington. Of sixteen male Carnegie trustees (there was only one woman, a member of the Carnegie family), twelve belonged to Century, and six belonged to either Metropolitan or Cosmos, or both. Allen W. Dulles also belonged to several of these clubs.

Kloby describes how this "cross-fertilization" worked in Guatemala, where in 1954 the CIA instigated a revolt against an elected reformer who had nationalized land owned by the United Fruit Company. The then U.S. secretary of state, John Foster Dulles, Allen W. Dulles's brother, had been legal counsel to United Fruit earlier on. By that time Allen was CIA director. He had been president of United Fruit. The U.S. ambassador to the United Nations, Henry Cabot Lodge, was on the board of directors of United Fruit.

The day after the CIA-sponsored invasion of Guatemala from Honduras, the Guatemalan government went to the UN Security Council to plead for action. The request was turned down by the president of the council, who was then Henry Cabot Lodge.[29] James D. Cockcroft summarizes: "The U.S. intervention was in direct response to an attempt by a constitutionally elected government to carry out its campaign promise to deliver uncultivated lands to impoverished peasants…[United Fruit] had no problem finding people to encourage and coordinate the intervention…."[30]

Today this kind of crude cause-and-effect relationship is disguised by laws forcing "public servants" to place their stock holdings into "blind trusts" on the assumption that this will insure their neutrality when it comes to decisions concerning their own corporate holdings. This is fostered by the naive assumption that people develop amnesia about their former property interests when they assume public office, and that their entire socialization into the capitalist value system similarly disappears.

There is a widespread impression that specific policies are determined by the state, acting in the interest of the larger society. The intermediate steps in the determination of state policy are often hidden, certainly from the public. But if we look at the lists of individuals actually involved in policy-making (in Carnegie's case, twelve of seventeen of its board of trustees in 1947 and 1948 were from leading corporate and financial institutions, and/or Wall Street "white shoe" law firms, and a thirteenth was the U.S. secretary of state, and in the Guatemalan case virtually the entire State Department leadership was or had been directly involved with United Fruit), Domhoff's argument that an upper-class perspective dominates broad governmental policy is overwhelmingly supported.

The biographies of major single actors are also illustrative of this general approach. The classic upper-class "public servant" in recent years may have been John J. McCloy (1895–1988), an "archetypical establishment figure," according to the *New York Times*. A member of several Wall Street law firms, McCloy served as assistant secretary of war from 1941–45, was president of the World Bank from 1947–49, military governor and high commissioner of Germany from 1949–52 (hence supervising West Germany's economic reconstruction), chairman of the board of the Council on Foreign Relations from 1953 to 1970 (preceding David Rockefeller), chairman of the President's Advisory Committee on Arms Control and Disarmament from 1961–74, a member of the Warren Commission, the chairman of the Ford Foundation from 1953–65, chairman of the board of Chase National Bank (later Chase Manhattan) from 1953–60, a director of the Dreyfus Corporation and Mercedes-Benz of North America, chairman of Squibb's Executive Committee, and, almost needless to say, a member of both the Century Club (New York) and the Metropolitan Club (Washington).[31] He was also involved with the boards of several colleges and universities.

But all this was long ago. Surely things are different, less corporate-determined now. Or are they? Those who have been following recent events involving lobbying efforts know better: there are, in Washington, D.C., some 1,700 "trade associations" constituting the capital's second-ranking private industry after tourism. Most promote business interests. One of the more influential lobbies is the Business Roundtable, consisting of about two hundred chief executive officers from some of the largest banks and corporations in the country. It was founded in 1973 by the heads of Alcoa and General Electric; subsequent presidents were from General Motors, DuPont, and Exxon. It played major roles in undermining consumer protection legislation in the mid-1970s, and in blocking reforms that would have given organized labor more rights.

In yet another example (the list could go on), there was the famous letter written by seven former defense secretaries to President Clinton in January 1995, advocating that B-2 bomber production not be terminated. Of those seven, six were by that time involved with firms doing "defense" business in some form, and the seventh was a "fellow" of the American Enterprise Institute, a right-wing think tank.

In power-structure research, when the emphasis is on individuals (the cross-fertilization idea), this can be called "subjectivist" instrumentalism, as in case studies of people, their family backgrounds, their memberships and organizational positons, or, as in the Guatemalan or B-2 bomber cases, how individuals exchange their positional hats. This is little more than old-fashioned muckraking. But when the emphasis is more on the interaction of *institutions*, as in the Harvard Russian Research Center affair, we are dealing with what can be called "structuralist" instrumentalism, or what Domhoff calls the "class dominance" perspective. He posits that "there is (1) a small social upper class (2) rooted in the ownership and control of a corporate community that (3) is integrated with a policy-planning network and (4) has great political power in both political parties and dominates the federal goverment in Washington."[32] So it is not a matter of individuals, but rather what they represent, as Kloby mentions. The evidence is that this "dominant class" is not completely unified. But although there are differences between different parts of this institutional network, and certainly between individuals, about all sorts of tactical questions, this interlocking system usually comes to a consensus on *broad* strategy, even though there continues to be disagreement on smaller-scale issues like the B-2 bomber. For example, there was disagreement, after World War II, as to which of several strategies were optimal to "deal" with the Soviet Union. But soon enough, utilizing such frameworks as the Council on Foreign Relations, a consensus around the so-called containment policy did develop.

The "ruling class," therefore, consists of a number of different elements or "fractions," which have somewhat differing short-term interests. Wall Street's internationally oriented financial and industrial capital, which tends to favor a *modus vivendi* with competing powers abroad, and prefers a "free trade" environment, versus more domestically oriented Middle Western and "Sunbelt" capitals, which prefer a more belligerent attitude toward foreign competition, and is more "protectionist" about international trade, is one of the clearer examples. This has sometimes been referred to as the "Yankee-Cowboy War."[33]

Another example has to do with the strategy of how to deal with domestic unrest. The Trilateral Commission, referred to in the previous chapter, consists of U.S., Western Europe, and Japanese establishment members, and was funded by David Rockefeller and others in the U.S. "Eastern Establishment." During the Carter administration the commission came out with several studies that pointed to the decreasing manageability of modern society due to an alleged collapse of traditional values and decreasing confidence in government, in short, a legitimation crisis expressed in conservative language. The authors of these studies, in line with the "friendly fascism" idea, called, among other things, for more economic planning in order to sustain prosperity, strengthening the hand of the state, and restricting some political freedoms. They emphasized close cooperation among the major capitalist powers, hence advocated a kind of capitalist international. "Because this perspective requires some sacrifice of short-term sovereignty and self-interest in exchange for long-range global planning," says Alan Wolfe, it is at variance with the laissez-faire, isolationist, and decentralist (anti-Washington) rhetoric of much of the Republican Party and some of the business elements that support it.[34] This dispute, which is really about the best way to keep the system on an even keel, continues among the various fractions of capital today, and is reflected in the debates within, and between, the major parties plus, on occasion, beyond them, as in the case of Ross Perot.

In the context of these internal disputes, the state sometimes appears to be an autonomous actor. Even more so, then, when a liberal (in the United States) or socialistic (in Europe) government is elected and proceeds to enact reforms that appear to constrain the corporate sector, or even to initiate popular redistributive policies like the graduated income tax. Pure instrumentalist or class dominance theory must then be amended in the direction of what is termed "relative autonomy" theory. There is a close connection between this idea, Whitt's notion of "class-dialectical" theory, and recent developments in the Marxist theory of the state.[35]

There are three interrelated aspects to this approach. One has to do with the function of the state as mediator of conflicts among and within classes. The second has to do with the function of the state as provider of services to the capitalist system. The third has to do with the inhibitions on state functioning that prevent it from being truly autonomous. In each of these dimensions, however, the state *appears* to be *relatively* autonomous, that is, it does not appear to be acting at the behest, or as an agent, of any individual corporate interest. In fact, it may act *against* a specific interest, as when a government briefly nationalizes railroads or coal mines. Rather, it acts on behalf of the entirety of the system. It often does so at social policy levels that appear quite unconnected to the direct interests of the system of private enterprise, much less of a specific industry. Let us examine each of these dimensions of the state's "relative autonomy."

"Today, as always," the Marxist Nicos Poulantzas told us, "the state plays the role of political unifier...and political organizer of the hegemony of monopoly capital within the power bloc, which is made up of several fractions of the bourgeois class and is divided by internal contradictions."[36] One fraction, that of the monopolistic or oligopolistic big businesses in the industrial and financial sector, however, does ultimately dominate. The state carries out this politically unifying mission by regulating the economy in such a way as to assure capital accumulation (profitability) for as many fractions as possible, but particularly for the hegemonic fraction. The survival and growth of big capital is ultimately the crucial element in the survival of most capital (not all, because some goes bankrupt in the process). The state also acts as a unifier, or promoter of consensus among the fractions of capital plus a few other elements that are not directly involved in business but have some political power in a modern democracy, such as organized labor. It does so through its very structure, which creates an arena (parliament, or congress) in which intrasystem disputes are debated and resolved in what appears to be a democratic, legitimate way (even though we know that these resolutions are often predetermined by backroom wheeling and dealing, and sometimes bought through outright corruption). And, most important, it does so by providing a set of infrastructural supports that, although they appear to be "neutral," actually function to assure the survival and legitimation of the system.

This is then the second function, that of providing services. There are several kinds of services: first, there is infrastructural support such as providing a central banking system, roads, railways, telecommunications including a postal system, power (dams, electricity), the promotion of certain kinds of research, etc. The Federal Aviation Administration, which operates airport control towers, is a prime example. It is this infrastructure that is the necessary condition for the development of a modern economy in the first place, whether that economy is capitalist, or not. Not all capitalist states organize all of these services, and even when they do, there is often pressure to "privatize" them when there is a prospect of turning them into profitable enterprises. Nevertheless, insofar as private capital is incapable or unwilling to provide these services, they must be provided on behalf of capital, with the costs "socialized," or spread around in the form of taxation on the entire population.

Another state service on behalf of capital is that of regulation for the sake of stability. Examples abound: the Interstate Commerce Commission, the Federal Trade Commission, the Securities Exchange Commission, the Federal Aviation Administration, etc. Even, or especially, when the state intervenes to protect the environment, imposes minimal housing requirements for farm laborers, increases the minimum wage, or (in the judicial system) allows juries to fine corporations for damaging people's health, it does so for the sake of stability, since such reforms preempt, or coopt, existing or potentially disruptive social movements. The kind of brutal intra-corporate competition in the early years of the industrial revolution, the era of the robber barons, needed to be made more civil and less chaotic. And the social movements of the Progressive Era also needed to be dampened down.

The legitimation problem requires reform. Domestic tranquility, as the Preamble to the U.S. Constitution says, is a fundamental goal of the state. One of the state's important services is to provide a certain level of social "net" in the form of welfare and a broad array of other social services, many of which were created in direct response to social protest movements. But when reform becomes too expensive, or too challenging to the prerogatives of big capital, the accumulation drive may require repression through police action. The so-called criminal justice system, therefore, is a twin to the social services provided by the state, the stick to the carrot.

One of the most important services of the state, regardless of the class system, is that of providing military "defense," or war-making capacity. Virtually without exception, and despite the usual rhetoric of acting in the *national* interest, the function of the military machine is to protect, or advance, the interest of the dominant class in whatever society, whether it be precapitalist, noncapitalist, or capitalist. Even what appears to be religious and ethnic strife ends up, at bottom, to be about the distribution of power, which includes power over economic resources such as land and other raw materials, within or among classes.

Finally, there is the service to the present system provided by the state in "the reproduction of the productive forces of the society (new workers), and in the reproduction of the social relations of production (the socialization process by which we become indoctrinated in the modes of behavior appropriate to our individual roles in the productive process)."[37] New workers have to be produced, first of all, biologically, so that the society must somehow create mechanisms such as the family, which must be provided with sufficient resources (like a minimum wage) to do that. But workers also need training to take their places in the contemporary labor market. This training takes two forms: first, technical training (computer literacy, mathematics, etc.), and, at higher levels, training for management and the professions, which may include some liberal arts. But a second kind of training is even more important: learning about how to behave appropriately in one's place in the system, or being socialized in a way appropriate to one's class standing. The "tracking system" in the formal educational structures of most countries segregates future workers more or less based on their parents' income and class, so that strata of workers are trained to take their places in the labor force. This is mainly done by what are called objective examinations, and this system pursues students from kindergarten through graduate and professional school. The examination system reproduces class differences. This mechanism of educational tracking is accompanied by socialization mechanisms that perform what Miliband called "an important class-confirming role."[38] Critics and educational innovators like Paolo Freire, Paul Goodman, and Carl Rogers long ago pointed out that the very structure of the classroom (students seated in rows, the lecture system, versus interactive "seminar" and student-centered learning) plays a very important role in the reproduction of social relations, which have less to do with technical know-how than with learning one's "place" in the class system, which is what social relations are about.[39] The state carries out both training and socialization functions for the larger system by underwriting education in general, and teacher and professor training in particular, and supporting this indirect subsidy to capital by passing these costs, too, on to the taxpayers. The legitimation function is supported by the rhetoric of local control of primary and secondary education (in the United States at least) and by "academic freedom," which permits limited amounts of deviant views to be expressed in higher education.

The third aspect of the "relative autonomy" approach deals with the problem of why the state cannot be autonomous, the inhibitions on the state (and its officials) even when it, or they, desire to enact reforms that might seriously challenge or undermine the power of capital. The first constraint on the state is that its social-policy choices are limited by previous developments in the economy. If the automobile industry has successfully eliminated public-streetcar systems due to its lobbying activities, the state must perforce build more and better roads. If automobiles become the only viable form of transportation, and roads and highways are built to accomodate them, then suburbanization and the decline of the city as an economic enterprise follow. The state (whether at the national or at the local level) must then respond to the needs and problems emanating from this urban-to-suburban shift. If "deindustrialization" undercuts the city's tax base, its infrastructure (education, social services, policing) suffers and creates political problems that must be coped with. Planning, as well as other social policies, whether successful or not, are state enterprises that constitute indirect responses to developments in the private economy. A reverse example is that of the nuclear industry: the state has had an interest in promoting this industry on the assumption that dependence on depletable resources such as coal or gas leaves a nation vulnerable. However, due to public protest and cost the industry (at least in the United States and Germany) has failed to take off, and the state has had to pull back.

A more important constraint on state managers is that of business confidence. "Business confidence falls during political turmoil, and rises when there is a restoration of order.... Since state managers are dependent upon the investment accumulation process, they will necessarily use whatever resources they possess to aid that process.... Dominant groups won't support state actions that aren't in their best interests, and state action cannot succeed without this support."[40] Even when powerful social movements are able to promote reforms, and these become part of state policy, "they are rarely granted in their original form. Rather, they are geared to the needs of capital accumulation."[41] (Domhoff cites New Deal agricultural policy, the National Recovery Administration, also under Roosevelt, and Social Security, among others;[42] Piven and Cloward discuss a range of welfare and other antipoverty measures;[43] Cockcroft analyzes immigration policy;[44] Quadragno also discusses Social Security.[45])

The Sherman Anti-Trust Act of 1890 provides an interesting historical example. President Theodore Roosevelt, the symbolic leader of the Progressive Era, forced John D. Rockefeller, arguably the richest man in the world, to split his Standard Oil Company into thirty-four different corporations in 1906, after muckrakers had gone after him. The U.S. Supreme Court did not confirm the action taken under the act for five more years. Rockefeller received shares in all of these new companies; by 1911 his fortune had doubled. The breakup of Standard Oil had little if any effect on oil prices.

The National Labor Relations Act of 1935 suggests one kind of amendment to instrumentalist theory, and a context in which the state can act with a greater degree of relative autonomy: when the dominant class is divided along fractional lines. Domhoff points out that since agricultural workers were excluded from the protections of the act, the agribusiness fraction of capital (including its supporters among Southern Democrats and Middlewestern Republicans in Congress) did not oppose the new law. Roosevelt was therefore able to put into place a reform that placated labor and solidified its support for his party.

A broad consensus within capital concerning foreign policy, as in the case of the containment policy during the Cold War, nevertheless permits the state considerable leeway about strategic and tactical options, so that the state appears to act in an autonomous way in the foreign policy area. These options are framed by a number of considerations independent of what the Council on Foreign Relations might think although we do not know that its leadership is not consulted. One is that the executive branch may lack accurate information about a foreign country that is perceived to be a competitor or a foe. For example, the real military strength of the Soviet Union was continually overestimated (which of course provided rhetorical ammunition for continued growth in "defense" spending). Then, there are the idiosyncratic factors related to decisions made by the U.S. president. That is, President Truman's decisions on the Berlin blockade, John F. Kennedy's concerning the Berlin Wall and during the Cuban missile crisis, or George Bush or Bill Clinton's actions during the Gulf War could just as readily gone in a different direction, with drastically different consequences, although these actions did have the overwhelming support of economic and political elites after the fact, and perhaps before. President Clinton's initiatives during the 1999 Kosovo Crisis, on the other hand, failed to secure a consensus. This very failure created a vacuum that allowed him a free hand, at least for a time.

Foreign-policy options that appear autonomous are in part based on the fact that these options have to be taken in response to what foreign actors do. Reactions must often be quick. One can speculate about whether, or how the cold war might have developed if Stalin had taken a different set of decisions in 1948 concerning the Berlin blockade or the coup in Czechoslovakia. Still, the actions were taken, and required responses that were largely independent of what "Wall Street" might have thought. Of course Wall Street pretty much agreed that just about every presidential decision made in these cases was the right one. But then so did everyone outside the small circles of the peace and leftist socialist movements, which were insignificant in the 1940s and 1950s.

There is one constraint that sometimes forces the state in a democratic society to act against the interest of the dominant class and even against its own interest. That is a (fairly rare) situation in which some pressure group, or perhaps one segment of capital (such as the press) promotes an ideological campaign that takes on a life of its own, and distorts the normal decision-making process. An example is the U.S. embargo against Cuba. This policy is clearly against the interest of capital, which seeks new avenues for investment. It is also against the interest of the state in its role as promoter of capital accumulation policies. Yet the state is stymied because for political reasons (some of its own making stemming from the days when rabid anti-Communism was an ideological bulwark for its policies, some due to political dependence on emigré-origin consituencies) it cannot forthrightly abandon the embargo. It was able to overcome political resistance to opening investment opportunities in the case of Vietnam because oppositional ideological forces were too weak.

In the Third World the most important constraint on what sometimes appears to be an "autonomous" state enacting reforms is the threat of a military coup backed by a local oligarchy and/or by foreign governments, in the interest of foreign investors. In the First World, although the threat of military coup is not unkown, "The threat of investment slowdowns and capital flight constantly hangs over any government embarking on a new policy of reform. Leftist governments are particularly dependent on economic growth in their attempts to expand the public sector."[46] John D. Stephens cites a number of instances, the most classical one taking place in France, during the Popular Front government headed by Leon Blum in 1936. But President François Mitterrand, also a social democrat, faced the same problem forty-five years later, and was soon forced to backtrack on a whole series of reforms that had been promised, and to some extent enacted, despite his reelection in 1988. The socialists were crushed in the 1992 and 1993 elections, at least in part because of their retreat from these reforms.

From the business point of view, the state is seen as relatively autonomous every time it engages in any redistributive fiscal policy, or in any public expenditure that is not directly beneficial to capital. The threat of capital flight, as Stephens points out, is sometimes offset by the threat of labor unrest, and reforms do get enacted in response to mass protest movements from below, even though, as Piven and Cloward put it, these "concessions are rarely unencumbered. If they are given at all, they are usually part and parcel of measures to reintegrate the movement into normal political channels and to absorb its leaders into stable institutional roles."[47] So in the long run these reforms actually do benefit capital in the sense that they help the system to survive, as Franklin Roosevelt understood very well.

The evidence is clear that there is a close relationship between the strength of labor movements (and their political parties) and the degree to which the welfare state can be expanded, and is able to sustain itself. After all is said and done, "the social and economic rights associated with the welfare state are products of class struggle." When the fascist alternative to reforms was defeated as the result of

World War II, "the bourgeoisie everywhere settled for a compromise,"[48] at least for a time.

It is this approach that underlies Whitt's "class-dialectical conception of power." This is fancy terminology for saying "Marxist." It is dialectical because it incorporates the concept of conflict. It "sees power as potentially available to the subordinate classes if they become sufficiently class-conscious and politically organized to wrest control or to challenge the control of the means of production."[49] Where instrumentalism, and even class-dominance theory, especially that version linked to the Marcusian analysis of friendly fascism, tends to view the power structure as virtually immune to significant resistance, dialectical theory leaves room for optimism.

But how well does class-dominance theory (especially that aspect of it focusing on the interpenetration between the corporate and state sectors) hold up in modern capitalist countries other than the United States? In the United States one constant over the years has been an informal arrangement involving the practice that public servants, whether elected or whether career civil servants, can switch over to a career in the private sector. Corporations enjoy having people aboard who know the workings of government and continue to have inside social contacts. Moreover, since many elected officials are lawyers to start with, they have transferrable skills. Similarly, as we have seen, a great number of corporate leaders join the government in some capacity, normally by appointment. This interpenetration of sectors is far less likely in many other countries. Although upper-level government officials and corporate leaders do share many social traits, not the least of which is a similar education in elite institutions (which goes a long way in creating a common value system), at the formal level business and governmental career "tracks" tend to be more clearly separated, say, in Britain or in Germany. A feudal tradition contributes to this separation: civil servants are servants of the state or the king, rather than of the electors, the "people." Also important is the fact that in a parliamentary system, cabinet officers are generally elected to parliament. Unlike in the

United States, they are rarely appointed from the outside, from the corporate sector, from organized labor, or from a farmers' lobby. They are therefore first and foremost politicians, whose successful career paths are established through political parties, not through private institutions. Some of these parties may be based on organized labor to some extent as in Britain, so that union leaders are occasionally elected to Parliament, but it is the rare corporate official who runs for public office.

So it would appear that the state is necessarily more autonomous. It is true that in the era of autocracy, or even of emperors with parliaments as in Germany or Austria-Hungary, the state had far more autonomy than today. But that was largely because the bourgeoisie was still relatively weak. The state was still more or less Bonapartist. The fact is that the modern state is completely hemmed in by the need to maintain business confidence, that is, do whatever is necessary to keep stock and bond prices stable in order not to risk capital flight. It does not matter whether the Treasury secretary comes directly from a Wall Street investment firm, from a university economics department, is a civil servant with a Ph.D. in economics, or, as in a parliamentary system, is part of the cabinet because he, or she, is a leading member of that elected parliamentary party.

The survival of the system requires economic policies maximizing "prosperity" in order to maintain general legitimacy even if, at times, such policies are painful for particular segments of society, or fractions of capital. The state, using such mechanisms as its central banking system and money-creating powers, or by intervening directly by buying or selling its own, or foreign, currencies, can manipulate interest rates (leading to more, or less, availability of credit and therefore affecting investment, employment, and the rate of inflation); strengthen or weaken its currency relative to other nations, affecting imports, exports, and the balance of trade; and, if sufficiently powerful, influence World Bank and IMF policies that in turn profoundly affect the economies of many nations.

Although the state appears to be an autonomous actor when it engages in these actions, economic policies are hardly neutral. They are based on more or less (sometimes considerably less!) intelligent and effective decisions made in the overall interest of national capital in the context of global capital. They are not made as if a nation's economic interest is insulated from the rest of the world. To the contrary, every decision and action is carefully evaluated as to its global implications, as it must be, since every national economy is part of a complex web of international economic relations. The notion of a state that is autonomous, that stands neutrally above such economic realities, that takes no part in the eternal struggle between those who have and want more and those who have little or nothing, is an illusion.

## NOTES

1. Ferdinand Lundberg, *The Rich and the Super-Rich* (New York: Lyle Stuart, 1968), 270.

2. Arnold M. Rose, *The Power Structure* (New York: Oxford University Press, 1967), 2.

3. Ralph Miliband, "Poulantzas and the Capitalist State," *New Left Review* 82 (November–December 1973): 85n., quoted in Peter J. Freitag, "Class Conflict and the Rise of Government Regulation," *Insurgent Sociologist* 12, no. 4 (Winter 1985): 52.

4. Theda Skocpol, "Bringing the State Back In: Strategies of Analysis in Current Research," in *Bringing the State Back In*, ed. Peter B. Evans, Dietrich Rueschemeyer, and Theda Skocpol (Cambridge: Cambridge University Press, 1985), 6.

5. Ralph Miliband, *The State in Capitalist Society* (New York: BasicBooks, 1969), 5. In the German original, the word is *verwaltet*, which can also be translated as "administering." Managing, or administering? The latter would seem somewhat less active.

6. For a good discussion of the rise of progressivism and its limitations, see Herman Schwendinger and Julia R. Schwendinger, *The Sociologists of the Chair* (New York: BasicBooks, 1974), esp. chaps. 17 and 18.

7. Robert A. Dahl, *Who Governs? Democracy and Power in an American City* (New Haven: Yale University Press, 1961).

8. Quoted in Miliband, *The State in Capitalist Society*, 2–3.

9. Ibid., 4.

10. Peter Bachrach and Morton S. Baratz, "Decisions and Nondecisions," *American Political Science Review* 57 (September 1963).

11. G. William Domhoff, *Who Rules America Now?* (New York: Simon & Schuster, 1983), 185.

12. Jerry Kloby, *Inequality, Power, and Development* (Amherst, N.Y.: Humanity Press, 1997), 85.

13. Domhoff, *Who Rules America Now?* 166–67.

14. Goeran Therborn, "What Does the Ruling Class Do When It Rules?" *Insurgent Sociologist* (Spring 1976).

15. E. Digby Baltzell, *The Protestant Establishment* (New York: Random House, Vintage, 1966), 7.

16. E. Digby Baltzell, *An American Business Aristocracy* (New York: Free Press, Macmillan, Collier Books, 1962), 48.

17. Dennis Gilbert and Joseph A. Kahl, *The American Class Structure*, 4th ed. (Belmont, Calif.: Wadsworth Publishing, 1993), 212.

18. C. Wright Mills, *The Power Elite* (London: Oxford University Press, 1956), 18.

19. Ibid., 9.

20. Ibid., 11.

21. C. Wright Mills, *The Causes of World War III* (New York: Ballantine Books, 1960).

22. Paul Sweezy, "Power Elite or Ruling Class?" in *C. Wright Mills and the Power Elite*, ed. G. William Domhoff and Hoyt B. Ballard (Boston: Beacon Press, 1968).

23. For further discussion of this point see G. William Domhoff, *The Power Elite and the State* (New York: Aldine de Gruyter, 1990), chap. 5.

24. For example: Robert F. Arnove, ed., *Philanthropy and Cultural Imperialism: The Foundations at Home and Abroad* (Boston: G. K. Hall, 1980); Beth Mintz, "The President's Cabinet, 1897–1972," *Insurgent Sociologist* 5, no. 3 (Spring 1975); Mark S. Mizruchi, *The American Corporate Network 1904–1974* (Beverly Hills, Calif.: Sage, 1982); Michael Parenti, *Democracy for the Few* (New York: St. Martin's Press, 1995); John Porter, *The Vertical Mosaic*

(Toronto: University of Toronto Press, 1970), which is about Canada; Laurence H. Shoup and William Minter, *Imperial Brain Trust: The Council on Foreign Relations and U.S. Foreign Policy* (New York: Monthly Review Press, 1977); Michael Useem, *The Inner Circle* (New York: Oxford University Press, 1984) and other work; Michael Wala, *The Council on Foreign Relations and American Foreign Policy in the Early Cold War* (Providence, R.I.: Berghahn, 1994); Special Issue on "Analyzing Power Structures," *Critical Sociology* 16, nos. 2–3 (Summer–Fall 1989).

25. Kloby, *Inequality, Power, and Development*, 89.

26. Domhoff, *The Power Elite and the State*, 108.

27. Martin Oppenheimer, "Footnote to the Cold War: The Harvard Russian Research Center," *Monthly Review* 48, no. 11 (April 1997).

28. G. William Domhoff, *State Autonomy or Class Dominance?* (New York: Aldine de Gruyter, 1996), 29.

29. Kloby, *Inequality, Power, and Development*, 89.

30. James D. Cockcroft, *Latin America* (Chicago: Nelson-Hall Publishers, 1996), 124.

31. *Who's Who in America*, 1984–1985.

32. Domhoff, *State Autonomy or Class Dominance?*, 18.

33. James Salt, "Sunbelt Capital and Conservative Political Realignment," *Critical Sociology* 16, nos. 2–3 (Summer–Fall 1989); see also Mike Davis, *Prisoners of the American Dream* (London: Verso, 1986).

34. Alan Wolfe, *The Limits of Legitimacy* (New York: Free Press, 1977), 325–30.

35. J. Allen Whitt, *Urban Elites and Mass Transportation* (Princeton, N.J.: Princeton University Press, 1982); Fred Block, "The Ruling Class Does Not Rule," in Marvin E. Olsen and Martin N. Marger, eds., *Power in Modern Societies* (Boulder, Colo.: Westview Press, 1993); Bob Jessup, *The Capitalist State* (New York: New York University Press, 1982); James O'Connor, *The Fiscal Crisis of the State* (New York: St. Martin's Press, 1973); Nicos Poulantzas, *Classes in Contemporary Capitalism* (London: Verso, 1978); Jill S. Quadragno, "Welfare Capitalism and the Social Security Act of 1935," *American Sociological Review* 49 (October 1984).

36. Poulantzas, *Classes in Contemporary Capitalism*, 157.

37. Martin Oppenheimer, *White Collar Politics* (New York: Monthly Review Press, 1985), 14.

38. Miliband, *The State in Capitalist Society*, 241.

39. Paulo Freire, *Pedagogy of the Oppressed* (New York: Herder and Herder, 1972); Paul Goodman, *Compulsory Mis-education and the Community of Scholars* (New York: Random House, Vintage, 1966); Carl R. Rogers, *On Becoming a Person* (Boston: Houghton Mifflin, 1961). See also Theodore Mills Norton and Bertell Ollman, *Studies in Socialist Pedagogy* (New York: Monthly Review Press, 1978).

40. Quadragno, "Welfare Capitalism and the Social Security Act of 1935," 633.

41. Ibid., p. 645.

42. Domhoff, *State Autonomy or Class Dominance*. See also the new edition of *Who Rules America?* (Mountain View, Calif.: Mayfield Publishing, 1998), 266–81.

43. Frances Fox Piven and Richard A. Cloward, *Regulating the Poor* (New York: Random House, Vintage, 1971).

44. James D. Cockcroft, *Outlaws in the Promised Land* (New York: Grove Press, 1986), chap. 5.

45. Quadrango, "Welfare Capitalism and the Social Security Act of 1935."

46. John D. Stephens, *The Transition from Capitalism to Socialism* (Urbana, Ill.: University of Illinois Press, 1986), 79, 160.

47. Frances Fox Piven and Richard A. Cloward, *Poor People's Movements* (New York: Random House, Vintage, 1979), 32.

48. Stephens, *The Transition from Capitalism to Socialism*, 197.

49. Whitt, *Urban Elites and Mass Transportation*, 22.

# 5

# THE FASCIST MOVEMENT AND THE FASCIST STATE

*Only under the second Bonaparte does the state seem to have made itself*
*completely independent. As against civil society, the state machine has*
*consolidated its position so thoroughly that the chief of the Society of*
*December 10 suffices for its head, an adventurer blown in from abroad,*
*raised on the shield by a drunken soldiery, which he has bought with*
*liquor and sausages, and which he must continually ply with sausage*
*anew. . . . And yet the state power is not suspended in midair. Bonaparte*
*represents a class. . . .*

    Karl Marx, *The Eighteenth Brumaire of Louis Bonaparte* [1]

Defining fascism, exploring theories of why and how it came into
being, and comprehending the nature of the fascist state is to
enter a social scientific and political minefield. The topic is controversial, to say the least. As the Belgian Trotskyist Ernest Mandel
observed in his introduction to Trotsky's essays on fascism, investi-
gations of fascism "generally support specific political conceptions
. . . the dominant interpretation of a certain historical event performs
a specific function in the developing social conflicts." [2] Not even the
definition of fascism, therefore, can be really value-neutral. The
second problem is that fascism does not fit into any prior system of

classifying movements and states. And yet fascism is arguably the most researched and theorized political phenomenon of the twentieth century, even including Soviet Communism. Still, the "Nazi Question," as one author has termed it, remains.[3]

The fascist state, following the conceptual framework outlined in chapter 1, arises when the bourgeoisie is *no longer* capable of ruling through a parliamentary state, the kind of state in which the various fractions of capital can come to a consensus about social policy by means of a "pluralism at the top." At the same time, alternative classes (especially the working class) have failed to carry out the kind of class revolution that would be required to supplant the bourgeoisie. The primary function of fascism is to rescue big capital by suppressing the Left, as well as subsidiary fractions of capital, but at the price of the destruction of the republican form of government. The appearance of state autonomy under fascism is belied by the reality of the continuation of the capitalist dynamic, even though that dynamic is severely regulated, especially by the regimentation required for the preparation for and the conduct of war. But that is true of parliamentary capitalist states in wartime also. Yet the appearance of autonomy is not completely false, either, for even though capitalism as a system is preserved, even promoted, individual capitalists and their firms prosper only insofar as they are able to demonstrate their loyalty to the fascist (or Nazi) regime and their willingness to subordinate their corporate agendas to its grandiose schemes, even when the program of the fascist state clearly endangers economic, and even military, efficiency. The two clearest examples of such policies were the Nazis' program of anti-Semitism, and Hitler's refusal to release many German women from their primary function in the household in order to aid the war effort more directly. The diversion of military forces to control forced labor in industry and to monitor concentration camps also turns out to be an inefficient use of resources.

What is unique about fascism and differentiates it fundamentally from the occasional coup d'etat by military officers disgusted by parliamentary chaos in the Third World, which reflects a bourgeoisie *not yet* capable of ruling, is that fascism comes to power through a mass movement that claims to be revolutionary. A wide array of observers over the years have accepted that claim. "Hitler no more questioned the revolutionary purpose and significance of the events he set in motion than had Jefferson, Robespierre, or Lenin before him," says historian David Schoenbaum, who believes that the Nazi's ideological revolution was *against* bourgeois and industrial society.[4] The revolution of nihilism, Hermann Rauschning called it. The revolt of the masses, said Ortega y Gasset. The Nazis' "complete revision of values *is* the Nazi Revolution," wrote social psychologist Hadley Cantril.[5] Yet in the classical sense of a displacement of one social and economic ruling class by another, the preponderance of the evidence tells us that it was not a revolution at all. As Leon Trotsky, writing in June 1933, put it, "The Nazis call their overturn by the usurped title of revolution. As a matter of fact, in Germany as well as in Italy, fascism leaves the social system untouched."[6] Following Mandel's logic, we need to ask what the function of claiming fascism to be revolutionary might be. Might it be that it helps sidetrack the idea that fascism is a *continuation* of capitalism, not a "revolutionary" break with it?

But if that is true, what is the meaning of the terms "socialist" and "worker" in the name National Socialist German Workers' Party (NSDAP in German, or Nazi for short)? Was this just empty rhetoric designed solely to attract mass support? Most historians conclude that it was more than that. Conversely, how do we explain Hitler's support among segments of the wealthy, given his revolutionary sloganeering? Was the Nazi Party a movement of the Left, or of the Right, both, or neither? And did the fascist state serve capital, the nation, itself only, or whom? For if one thing is certain, it did not serve the working class of Germany or Italy, which had to pay for the policies of their fascist states by extreme exploitation in the factory, deprivation in daily life, and blood on the battlefield. Nor did it serve "the nation," if by that we mean the general population which was, in any case, predominantly working class or peasant. How was it possible first to dupe, then to mobilize the German (or the Italian, or other) population against its own best interest?

First, not everyone was duped. In the July 1932 German parliamentary election, the Nazi vote stood at 13.7 million, a plurality, but not a majority. The Communists and Socialists together garnered 13.2 million, with almost 3 million for various center parties. This was the high watermark of Nazi voter support. Even after Hitler came to power and had begun the terrorization of opposition elements, the Communists and Socialists still received over 12 million votes against the Nazis' 17.2 million in the March 1933 election. Hitler then had the eighty-one Communist and numerous Socialist deputies arrested, and then a rump parliament voted itself effectively out of business on March 24 1933 to begin the process of the consolidation of the Nazi state.

At the other end of the class spectrum, the wealthy were not duped either, if we interpret their disproportionate vote for Hitler as a vote for stabilizing capitalism and suppressing the Left. In a study of fourteen of Germany's largest cities, Richard Hamilton correlates the class composition of city districts with their party votes. "Support for the National Socialists in most cities varied directly with the class level of the district. The 'best districts' gave Hitler and his party the strongest support...."[7] Yet the upper-income strata, being a small minority, could hardly have been responsible for the Nazi's electoral successes. Large proportions of lower-middle-class, white-collar and blue-collar workers also voted for Hitler's party (the proportion declining as income declined). Still, more than one-fourth of the working class supported the Nazis in 1932.

Theories about fascism as a movement are concerned primarily with who backed the Nazis and why, and range from purely psychological approaches to the institutional and historical theses of a variety of Marxist schools. Theories of fascism as a state are concerned mainly with two issues: the state's degree of autonomy, and the state's degree of totality, or "totalitarianness."

The most general theory attempting to explain the attraction of fascism to so many people is the "mass society" idea, expounded in various forms by both conservatives and some leftists. In this view, the development of modern, bureaucratic society has destroyed the bonds that tie people to community, family, church. More and more people are torn from their cultural roots and become isolated, "disintegrated" due to the transition from rural to urban life, and the constant need for geographical movement in the quest for employment. Traditional social institutions that provided a stuctured and generally accepted set of values are undermined, resulting in "social atomization and extreme individuation," so that the population becomes one undifferentiated mass: "[T]he masses grew out of the fragmentation of a highly atomized society.... The chief characteristic of the mass man [sic] is ... his isolation and lack of normal social relationships," Hannah Arendt wrote.[8] Post–World War I European society especially suffered from a cultural meltdown, as monarchies toppled, returning veterans confronted political and economic chaos and unemployment, and inflation and depression bankrupted small businesses and farmers. Prior cultural norms now made no sense; the condition called *anomie,* or normlessness, culminating in personal or psychological disorganization, became common. In seeking a solution to the confusions resulting from this new kind of freedom (from tradition and community) the individual, according to Erich Fromm, himself a social democrat, seeks an "escape from freedom" in submission to and membership in a "pseudocommunity": the mass movement and the totalitarian leader.[9]

Conservative or aristocratic critics of this "mass society" such as Hermann Rauschning and Jose Ortega y Gasset viewed the twentieth century with considerable alarm because they believed that the movements resulting from the breakdown of traditional structures were attaining social and political power. This "revolt of the masses" was one of destruction, of terroristic immorality, in short, a floodtide of nihilism, as Nietzsche said. "When the mass acts on its own, it does so only in one way, for it has no other: it lynches.... When the mass triumphs, violence triumphs."[10] The roots of fascism (as well as other totalitarian movements such as communism) are among the uprooted and disinherited of all social and economic classes. The mass-society school posits that disgruntled war veterans, un- and underemployed intellectuals, the lumpenproletariat, the lower middle class of small shopkeepers and farmers, and marginal fractions of big business form the base of support for Nazism, particularly its uniformed cadres, the very large group of individuals marginal to, or excluded from what remains of mainstream society. This is obviously a fearful prospect for traditional aristocrats and conservatives who see themselves as the guardians of civilized society, and the mass of the population as incapable of directing society and eternally vulnerable to the manipulation of demagogues. It is unquestionably true that significant elements of the German upper class shared this view and saw Hitler as a "brown bolshevik" (after the color of the shirts of his stormtroopers), a crude upstart whom they feared only slightly less than they feared communism. Yet it was one of their own, the revered president and general von Hindenburg who appointed Hitler chancellor (in effect prime minister) on January 30, 1933.

Democratic critics of mass society agree that modern society has undermined what is called *civil society*, those institutions that mediate between people and the larger system. But that system has a name: capitalism. Franz Neumann, for example, tells us that "the transformation of men [*sic*] into mass-man is the outcome of modern industrial capitalism...."[11] What fascism does, in his view, is to carry this transformation "to its highest perfection" in that it "has annihilated every institution that under democratic conditions still preserves remnants of human spontaneity: the privacy of the individual and of the family, the trade union, the political party, the church," thereby helping to consolidate the ruling class in its domination of the subordinate strata. Erich Fromm did not disagree. But he insisted that while "Nazism is an economic and political problem...the hold it has over a whole people has to be understood on psychological grounds" as well. Yet "the psychological factors themselves have to be understood as being molded by socio-economic factors."[12]

Fromm believed that the societal breakdown following World War I created conditions for the growth of a personality type that was impelled towards authoritarian causes, and that Nazi propaganda consciously or unconsciously fed into the needs of this personality type for identification and security. This type he called the *sado-masochistic* personality. This personality needs to "escape from freedom" by giving up "the independence of one's own individual self and to fuse one's self with somebody or something outside of oneself in order to acquire the strength which the individual self is lacking."[13] The sadist, by making other persons suffer, demonstrates his power over them, while the masochist submits himself to suffering. In either case, the individual engages in a process that Fromm designates as "symbiosis," or the union of the self with another self or another power, thus enabling the self to reassert itself, to gain some form of stability or security in that identification. The success of the charismatic leader, of mass meetings and nationalistic sloganeering, are evidence of the individual's projection of personal fate to the fate of the nation. The masochist's submission to the leader and to the national fate is an adjustment to individual failure, while the destructive, sadistic personality escapes a feeling of powerlessness in being destructive. There is always the need to look for some higher power to which one can submit. Hitler regularly referred to his aims in terms of higher powers even than himself: God, Fate, History, Nature, National Instinct, etc.

Fromm's approach is closely linked to the idea of the "authoritarian personality," a concept made famous by the exiled Frankfurt sociologist T. W. Adorno and others.[14] Adorno's well-known "F-Scale" purports to measure the propensity toward authoritarianism, in which he includes submission (uncritical attitudes toward the moral authority of the in-group); aggression (the tendency to condemn, reject, and punish people who violate conventionalities); opposition to the subjective, the imaginative, the tender-minded;

superstition (the belief in mystical determinants of fate); power and toughness, destructiveness, cynicism; projection (the disposition to believe that wild and dangerous things go on in the world); and perhaps most important, the propensity to see the world in either-or, black-white, good-evil terms, sometimes called *Manicheanism*. The classical F-Scale kind of question asks the respondent to agree or disagree in various degrees with the statement that what your country needs is a strong and fearless leader to clean up the mess, a constant in the message of all demagogues.[15] The healthy or democratic personality, on the other hand, is prepared to deal with grays, with ambiguities, and to trust in democratic problem-solving processes.

One problem, however, with the authoritarian personality studies, as well as with most discussions of "mass man" and "mass movements," is that no distinction is made between them: all charismatic leaders, all mass movements, all shirt colors are the same. Clearly this is not true. There are vast differences between movements that are fundamentally inclusive and democratic and those that are xenophobic and dictatorial. Even the parallels often drawn between Nazism and Communism are overdrawn, for at least in rhetoric and historical tradition the latter has its roots in the Western Enlightenment tradition, and in day-to-day practice (at least outside the former Soviet bloc) was antiracist and adhered to some minimal democratic procedures.

Wilhelm Reich, expelled from the German Communist Party for his extreme psychological theories, took the ideas of Fromm, Adorno, and others further, although he actually preceded them chronologically. In his view, first expressed in 1933 and not published in English until 1946, "[T]here is today not a single individual who does not have the elements of fascist feeling and thinking in his (sic) structure. ... '[F]ascism' is the basic emotional attitude of man in authoritarian society, with its machine civilization and its mechanistic-mechanical view of life....In its pure form, fascism is the sum total of all *irrational* reactions of the average human character."[16] For Reich, sexual repression, the product of religiosity, patriarchy, and political and economic authoritarianism of all kinds (including in the Soviet Union), generates mysticism and the longing for authority that in turn reproduces the "helpless and authoritarian character structure of the masses of people." Thus "German fascism was born from the biological rigidity . . . of the former generation. Prussian militarism, with its machine-like discipline, its goose-step . . . is the extreme manifestation of this biological rigidity. . . . It is clear: social freedom and self-regulation are inconceivable in rigid, machine-like people."[17] For Reich, the authoritarian personality is linked to the repressive social structures that suppress sexual expression, beginning in infancy within the authoritarian family. But since virtually everyone in Western society, capitalist or not, is to some extent sexually repressed from infancy on, the question remains as to the circumstances under which these distorted personalities can be mobilized for a fascist movement that, even in Reich's thinking, serves reactionary ends. Although repressive, even violent, family behavior is important as a predictor of authoritarian tendencies, are there not mediating factors of a social and institutional kind that are more important?

Nazi propaganda emphasized a number of themes common in varying degrees to ultraconservative, nationalistic, and fascist movements in other countries, including in contemporary "ultra" movements such as the U.S. "militia" movement. The most common feature of all these movements is a supernationalism in which the presumed glories of the past are to be restored and the nation, people, or "Volk" made whole again. This message is combined with a distrust of current parliamentary governments that have allegedly betrayed the nation in some way (as in losing a war). The disastrous Versailles Treaty, despised by all sectors of German society, and which saddled Germany with extortionate reparations payments and the loss of territory, provided ample ammunition for Hitler's nationalistic propaganda. This theme emphasizes the unity of the people (as against the divisive class-struggle messages of the Left). A second theme common to such movements (excepting conservatives) is a populistic message targeting some sort of financial conspiracy (such as Wall Street) as being responsible for economic ills, and promising better days for "the little man" and "the people." A third theme is that of the "Führer" or leadership principle: a strong, incorruptible leader or savior in whom the people must trust is the way out.

Beyond those themes, a number of writers (including most of those discussed in this chapter) have pointed to the irrational or emotional component of fascist "thought," an idea fully embraced by fascists themselves. Here is Alfredo Rocco, theoretician of Italian fascism: "Fascism is, above all, action and sentiment and that it must continue to be.... Only because it is feeling and sentiment, only because it is the unconscious reawakening of our profound racial instinct, has it the force to stir up the soul of a people and to set free an irresistible current of national will."[18] This emotional component, closely linked to religiosity, nationalist fervor, submission to the leader, and immersion in the pseudocommunity of the movement, is the core of fascist appeal.

This places fascism in the same camp of antimodernity as the fundamentalist religions now sweeping the world. The movements with which fascism had to contend, including liberals, the Communists, and most mainstream conservatives, were all movements in the tradition of modernity, of the Enlightenment, rooted historically in the bourgeois American and French Revolutions. Whether one advocates capitalism or socialism, both are linked to the ideas of progress, industrialization, urbanization, science, and rational thought. Both are necessarily in opposition to superstition, theology, and irrationality. Fascism on the other hand constitutes a revolt against the Enlightenment and the project of modernity, against intellectualism, rationality, and the progress that has resulted in the breakdown of traditional communities and the patriarchal family, in alienation, isolation, and the collapse of traditional values. As Rocco said, "Fascism has not been wholly successful with the intellectual classes (because of the fixity of their aquired rational culture).... [I]t has been very successful with young people, with women, in rural districts, and among men of action unencumbered by a fixed and set social and political education." For Rocco, liberalism tends to isolate the present from the past, "destroying the unity and spiritual life itself of human society." By contrast, "Fascism is, above all, action and sentiment...force to stir the soul of a people...."[19]

When the themes of national or "Volk" unity, financial conspiracy, and antimodernity are combined, the result is a formula that logically makes anti-Semitism fundamental to fascism. The fact that fascisms other than the Nazi version may have been less anti-Semitic only demonstrates their deviation from the ultimate model. It was clear to the Nazis that the Jew was "the quintessentially modern man—urban, rootless, rational, immersed in the 'inauthentic' realm of commercial exchange. In a sense, the war to exterminate the Jews marked the ultimate extension of one form of antimodernism."[20] It was this broad theme of antimodernity, combined with the appeal of the pseudocommunity of movement and nation, that attracted (and continues to attract) so many of the psychologically homeless victims of modern society, and accounts for the persistence of anti-Semitism, "the socialism of fools."

Over the years, the thesis of the anomic, "mass-man" character of the Nazi supporter has been questioned by a large number of studies. The Nazis successfully appealed to many small-town, rural, and small proprietor voters who were neither rootless nor marginal. "The ideal-typical Nazi voter in 1932 was a middle-class self-employed Protestant who lived either on a farm or in a small community, and who had previously voted for a centrist or regionalist political party strongly opposed to the power and influence of big business and big labor."[21] The data that support this generalization, said sociologist S. M. Lipset, "sharply challenge the various interpretations of Nazism as the product of the growth of anomie and the general rootlessness of modern urban industrial society."[22] In fact, the larger the city, the smaller the proportion of Nazi voters. Moreover, it can hardly be argued that those elements of the upper middle and upper class that supported Hitler were lost souls suffering from anomie, although Nazi electoral support among the

upper strata was stronger among "provincial aristocratic and bourgeois elements that lacked control of the central machinery of government," rather than among core groups of the ruling class.[23] A
number of community studies have also pointed to the "normalcy"
of Nazi supporters.[24] It is true, however, that various indices of mar-
ginality were comparatively stronger among the *leaders*, the elite, of
the Nazi Party.[25]

The theme of antimodernity, on the other hand, has held up
pretty well. Yet this antimodern movement created a state that was
the very incarnation of modernity, at least superficially: the totalitarian bureaucracy that was able to organize a modern capitalist
society into an efficient military fighting machine that conquered
most of Europe, and with utter industrial efficiency, managed to
exterminate some six million Jews and several hundreds of thousands, if not millions, of other "undesirable" elements. Hitler's state
created the opposite of what he had promised the rural and small-
town petty bourgeoisie: The cities became larger, the concentration
of capital and the inequality of incomes greater, the rural population smaller, the Junkers still ran big agriculture, and the army continued to be led "by generals whose names began with 'von.' "[26] The
Nazi state was the state of the antimodern modernizers.

The class basis of the Nazi state (as distinct from the class base
of the Nazi movement) has been the subject of controversy for a
very long time, even before January 30, 1933, the day on which
Hitler was named chancellor. Over time, two theories have lost credibility. One is the simplistic, allegedly Marxist thesis of the Communist International and its sympathizers (from 1928 well into the
1930s and even later) that fascism is simply the "terroristic dictatorship of big capital,"[27] an undifferentiated "business enterprise organized on a monopoly basis, and in full command of all the military,
police, legal, and propaganda power of the state."[28] The other is its
opposite, that the Nazi state was, or in the course of the later 1930s
became, a state quite independent of the old German ruling class. In
this thesis German capital was from the beginning a distinctly sec-

ondary factor in putting Hitler into power, and after 1933 was, or soon became, a helpless tool in an agenda determined by Hitler.

The first thesis is rooted in a conspiratorial version of the idea that fascism constitutes a *continuation* of capitalism, capitalism's final gasp. The second is based on the idea that fascism is a revolutionary *break* from capitalism as we know it in the twentieth century, the consequence of specific weaknesses (the weak framework of the Weimer constitution, Germany's underdeveloped democratic tradition, errors of judgment, etc.). One is an indictment of the capitalist class in its entirety, the other a pardon for that class in its relationship to Nazism. The truth, insofar as it can be established given the many vested interests involved in this dispute, is somewhere in between, certainly somewhat more in the direction of the former theory, but the precise location in between is still the subject of great debate.[29]

The thesis of the Communist or Third International (the Comintern) as it developed in the 1920s was that the Nazi movement was at once a symptom of capitalism in acute crisis, and an instrument of big business. Hitler, should he come to power, would quickly demonstrate his incapacity for solving the crisis. His electoral success would boomerang, the system would fall into shambles, and the way would open for a Communist triumph. The tragically famous expression was, "after Hitler, us." The German Communist Party, reflecting similar policies promoted by Stalin in other branches of the Third International, considered the mass German Social Democratic Party scarcely better than the Nazis, indeed in some ways worse given its reformist, that is, nonrevolutionary and class collaborationist, character. The Social Democrats were attacked as "social fascists," and an alliance with them was considered unacceptable.

The Communists' thesis was not accepted uncritically even within the Third International, at least at first. As early as 1923, Klara Zetkin, a close friend of Rosa Luxemburg and a high official of the Comintern at the time, called for a united front of workers regardless of party affiliation, but within a few years she would lose influence. Following the expulsion of the Trotskyist Left Opposition from Communist Parties around the world, this tendency became significant in challenging the Stalinist theory about fascism from a leftist perspective. Trotsky called for a united front of the Communists with the Social Democratic Party, "embracing the entire proletariat" to struggle directly against fascism. He accused the German Communist Party of seeing Hitler as the lesser evil compared to the bourgeois republic, and of accepting the inevitability of a Nazi triumph in the illusion that Hitler would collapse in short order. In no way did Trotsky share the Communist Party's optimism about "after Hitler, us." He anticipated that a long and painful road lay ahead for the German proletariat, and in November 1933, further predicted that the "date of the new European catastrophe will be determined by the time necessary for the arming of Germany."[30]

Trotsky's view differed from that of the official Communists mainly in that he saw fascism as a far greater threat to the working class than did the Communists, so that he consequently proposed a strategy that would maximize working-class opposition to the Nazis. However, he, too, saw fascism as basically an instrument of big business in a time of crisis:

At the moment that the 'normal' police and military resources of the bourgeois dictatorship, together with their parliamentary screens, no longer suffice to hold society in a state of equilibrium—the turn of the fascist regime arrives. Through the fascist agency, capitalism sets in motion the masses of the crazed petty bourgeoisie, and bands of the declassed and demoralized lumpenproletariat....After fascism is victorious, finance capital gathers into its hands...all the organs and institutions of sovereignty....[31]

Trotsky believed that Germany's economic situation in the context of the world depression no longer left room for the kinds of concessions to the working class that were advocated by Social Democracy and that functioned to ward off revolution. "As Social

Democracy saved the bourgeoisie from the proletarian revolution, fascism came in its turn to liberate the bourgeoisie from the Social Democracy. Hitler's coup is only the final link in the chain of counterrevolutionary shifts."[32] In this view, too, Hitler was ultimately the instrument or lackey, with capital acting as the paymaster that bankrolled the Brownshirts.

More recent Marxist analyses put more emphasis on differentiating among the fractions of capital, and assessing more precisely who supported Hitler. The literal paymaster, the instrumentalist idea that Hitler acted *at the behest* of capital, was supplanted by the thesis that Hitler functioned *on behalf* of capital in a more general way, for the benefit of the overall system in a particular historical moment. Such an argument is made by Kurt Gossweiler, who begins by pointing to a fundamental problem in Weimar Germany: in order to overcome its economically crippled condition after the First World War, capital required an exploitation and subjugation of labor that was not possible given the democratic rights that had been won in 1918. The contradiction between the "social structure of the Weimar Republic, with its semi-feudal residues, and the bourgeois-democratic state form needed to be overcome."[33] The consequence was a political struggle to undermine the Weimer Republic that ultimately served economic ends. By 1930 the Nazi Party had become a major force "that opened up quite new, surprising, and welcome possibilities for overcoming the parliamentary obstacles for the 'legal' transition to a dictatorial form of domination."[34] Gossweiler argues that "the top levels of the most important German companies, the leaders of the landed aristocracy, and the Reichswehr generals" made the political decision to establish a fascist dictatorship. They "agreed, despite their internal conflicts, not to allow a return to the parliamentary system."[35]

A more widely accepted view among Marxists in recent years is that of David Abraham, who argues that it was precisely because of its sharpening internal conflicts that no one fraction of capital was able to dominate the others, or to build a stable parliamentary coalition, so that the Weimar Republic became inadequate to deal with current problems, especially in the context of the expensive social reforms extorted by the Social Democratic Left as its price for supporting the continuation of (a reformed) capitalism. Abraham points to heavy industry as being the key fraction providing support for the Nazi Party and urging the various bourgeois political parties to entertain cooperation with Hitler. "By mid-1932 the vast majority of industrialists wanted to see Nazi participation in the government... [T]he leading figures in the now decisive fraction of industry concluded that Nazi participation in or control of the government would provide the best way out of the political crisis while providing auspicious possibilities for a profitable economic recovery."[36] It was widely believed in elite circles that the Nazi movement could be "tamed" by means of cooperation and financial support, or that the Hitler dictatorship would only be a temporary expedient to discipline labor and stabilize the government.

While scholars such as Gossweiler argued that capitalism, broadly speaking, deliberately chose to subvert its parliamentary state and opt for a fascist solution, Neumann's earlier pioneering work was somewhat more deterministic. He believed that historical circumstances made it virtually impossible for the Weimar Republic to survive, and that the development of fascism was all but inevitable. How was the agenda of rebuilding Germany after the war to be accomplished? It could be done with foreign assistance, which was the preference of many liberals at the time. However, this was not supported very widely within Germany, nor could much aid be forthcoming from the West, which had its own economic problems. It could be done if the German elite were to make serious concessions in the way of income redistribution, hence generating purchasing power at the expense of profit. The elite was not open to this approach. It could be done by transforming the society into a socialist one, and expropriating large enterprises, but that too was excluded since the Social Democratic Party, certainly its leadership and parliamentary delegates, had long since given up being real socialists, and the Communists alone would have been insufficient, even had Stalin permitted such a development independent of Communist control. The only other alternative was imperialist expansion, which necessitated the mobilization and disciplining of the population. Only the Nazis appeared capable of carrying out this agenda. This was the therapy chosen, and supported both financially and politically, by large segments of German capital.

The most common criticism of this approach is that the evidence of capitalist backing for the Nazis is mixed, or of minimal importance. Even if the old German ruling class, or some elements of it, suffered from the illusion that they would be able to control Hitler, this illusion would soon be dispelled, and at some point (the date is debated) Hitler took full charge. The German capitalists, in this thesis, were naive, and a few did foolishly support the Nazis. But after 1933 their support was coerced. The Hitler regime ruled independently of (and sometimes against) capital. Konrad Heiden's position, in one of the pioneering studies of the Nazi movement, is typical. He argues that "contrary to widespread legend this [support by industry] was out of the question from 1925 to 1929—even later. The German economy did not raise up Hitler. He is no creature of money.... Actually, the funds [of industry] were attracted by success, rather than the other way around."[37]

It is clear that the Nazis (and later their regime) cannot be reduced to being simply the carefully contrived tool of a homogeneous and Machiavellian capitalist class. The evidence concerning which fraction of capital (including agriculture) supported the Nazis, and when, is somewhat ambiguous, with different scholars using different measures. For instance, capital in its various fractions supported a number of center and center-right nationalist parties rather than the NSDAP as late as March 1933. Most German capital stood with Marshall von Hindenburg in the elections of 1932, and not with Hitler. The amounts of money given by various individual capitalists, and their timing, and how to interpret this support is open to debate. Fritz Thyssen, a Ruhr industrialist who arranged some meetings between some of his group and Hitler in 1928, claimed he gave Hitler only one million gold marks between 1927 and 1933. He fled Germany in 1938. Did German capital really want a dictatorship of Hitler, or just a return to autocracy, with Hitler being only the temporary means? Did not many elements of German capital fear the populist, anticapitalist slogans of the "Brown Bolsheviks"? Was their support for Hitler really only indirect, in that they helped undermine the democratic institutions of Weimar? And who, exactly, were the "they"?

Two scholarly works exemplify the dilemma. David Abraham's *The Collapse of the Weimer Republic*, which presents a thorough breakdown of which fractions of capital did what prior to 1933, represents the view that German capital did see the Nazis as the way out of Germany's political crisis, and did support him directly or indirectly.

The contrasting view is that of the historian Henry A. Turner Jr., who claims that German industrialists gave money to moderate elements in the Nazi movement only so as to strengthen their position against the "radical" (populist) wing of the NSDAP, that much of their funding was really an "insurance policy" to protect them should Hitler come to power, and more generally that German big business had a lot less to do with Hitler's rise to power than is generally believed.[38] In the summer of 1997 Turner addressed the Twentieth Congress of the German Society for Entrepreneurial History, and was quoted to the effect that although German employers were fellow-travelers of Hitler, they were substantially no different than any other occupational group. He and other contributors to this meeting also downplayed German industry's later collaboration with the Hitler regime as it proceeded to mobilize the economy for war, including the use of concentration-camp inmates as slave labor. Although Turner's work has been favorably reviewed by some historians (as has Abraham's), Gossweiler dismisses it as being "in sharp contradiction to historical truth and [having] nothing whatsoever to do with scholarship."[39] It seems hardly debatable that the mid-1930s in Germany saw a significant growth in monopoly capital, summarized by Franz Neumann, who concluded that "Entrepreneurial initiative is not dead; it is as vital as ever before and perhaps even more so."[40]

Taken to its logical conclusion, Turner's thesis leads to the idea of the "primacy of politics," or the "state autonomy thesis." This broad view comes in a number of versions. One is that totalitarianism is a system that utilizes its unifying message and repressive political apparatus to fuse all classes into one mass so that the capitalist class as traditionally understood no longer exists, or if it exists, it does so at the pleasure of the dictator. Movements based on the disintegration of civil society hence lead to states that abolish most signifiers of class and class privilege. The common or mass man comes to power (in the guise of the Brown or Blackshirts) in a nation that rapidly becomes mobilized for combat. A more popular version goes a step further to argue that in this context it is possible for a madman such as Hitler to assume total control and frighten everyone, including the old ruling class, into submission. The factory is yours, said one journalist at the time, but the state tells you what to make, in what quantity and quality, and it provides raw materials and handles the markets. Another summarized the situation by observing that all capital was, simply, at the immediate disposal of the Nazi state. A more sophisticated version stated that Hitler's autonomy from the old ruling class was due to the complete incapacity of that class to come to any agreement about policy, so that the political disintegration of the ruling class (which actually preceded 1933) left a vacuum. Even if industry benefited disproportionally from the new state of affairs, such results were incidental or accidental, outcomes due to the requirements of an armaments economy that in turn was the fruit of fascist ideology, not of rational capitalist calculation.

The French Marxist Nicos Poulantzas integrated many of these ideas into a single framework in his much discussed book *Fascism and Dictatorship*.[41] Fascism, said Poulantzas, is but one form of "exceptional capitalist state" (another being Bonapartism; there are others as well) that correspond to different kinds of crisis. It arises when the domination (or hegemony) of big monopoly capital within a political alliance or "bloc" of other fractions of capital collapses due to "contradictions" within the bloc. These contradictions, or sharp differences in economic and political interests, were very clear in Weimar Germany: they are documented in Abraham's work, which is somewhat in Poulantzas's tradition, although Abraham does not explicitly refer to him. The function of fascism is then to suppress the political expression of these contradictions (an impotent parliament, which reflected the allegiance of various fractions of capital to a variety of center and right-center parties) and restore big capital to its dominant position within the wider capitalist bloc. Of course fascism also suppresses the political expression of other classes, especially the working class. This task enables the fascist state to be relatively autonomous, to stand above the fray and determine the course of events. Jane Caplan summarizes Poulantzas's central thesis: "that fascism's historic function is the performance of a service of mediation to monopoly capital, which it achieves partly by means of preserving its relative autonomy from capital."[42]

But there are flaws in this argument. One is that it assumes a unified command, a totalitarian state with a single policy, namely to restore representatives of the big bourgeoisie to their status as a ruling class on the political scene, in the state. But as Caplan points out, "... [R]esearch into the workings of Nazi government strongly suggests that it was characterized by an extreme diffusion...of authority, and a highly disordered proliferation of agencies and hierarchies."[43] The Nazi regime was an empire of constantly squabbling fiefdoms, sometimes called polycracy, barely held together by Hitler. Its policy vacillated over the years, purging first its own radical wing in 1934, and later some conservative politicians and old-line generals, though not as bloodily. After 1938, Caplan believes, the Nazi state's role became stronger, and the state became more autonomous. This led to a second problem: The fascist state had its own contradiction, which inevitably led to its downfall. The Nazis extensive apparatus of repression, combined with its military expansionism, meant that the processes of production and of the reproduction of labor and the relations of production (including an appropriate educational plant) were subverted. As politics (meaning the NSDAP, its structure, and its ideology) became more determining, the contradiction between it and the activities needed for capitalism to survive economically deepened. "... [T]he executions mount, the concentration camps fill, the police system takes off into total independence, and, at the most extreme and comprehensive level, war engulfs society, as the Nazi regime 'matures' into the full expression of its contradictions."[44] Poulantzas's view of fascism as leading to a reestablishment of the domination of capital cannot account for the collapse of fascism, which is the consequence of the contradictions generated by the disproportional strength, if not necessarily domination, of politics.

The difficulties these contradictions present for scholars are exemplified in trying to understand Hitler's foreign policy. This appeared to move in stages dependent somewhat on which elements of the old power structure he needed at a particular time. The attack on the Soviet Union in 1941, agreed to by Hitler's generals on the basis that it would be another "lightning war," soon became a "racial war" as increasing power was given to the SS, Hitler's elite troops. This symbolized, perhaps, the increasing autonomy of the Nazi state. Then Russian resistance stiffened, partisans joined in, and soon the German generals began to clash with Hitler on military strategy. But it was too late. Yet although the war was always in Hitler's plans, it is still not clear whether initially this was in order to solve the domestic crisis, or that he blundered into conflict with Great Britain in 1939 contrary to his intentions. "The link between expansionism and the defense of the status quo," as Pierre Ayçoberry puts it, is still a problem for scholars of the Third Reich.[45] Expansionism for whose benefit? The defense of whose status quo? The answers are still not clear.

Was fascism a creature of German capital, no matter how indirectly and generally, or was it largely autonomous? The most reasonable answer to this much-debated and still controversial question is that Abraham (and indirectly Poulantzas and some other Marxists) are right for the period up to about 1934 (according to some data) or at the latest 1938. Later, the Nazi state become more and more autonomous and polycentric, with Hitler as final arbiter. Even then, however, capitalist firms were implicated in varying degrees in all of Hitler's projects, from war production to concentration and extermination camps. Ultimately the catastrophe confronting Germany generally, and German capital specifically, led to the attempt on Hitler's life on July 20, 1944; its failure condemned Germany (and its concentration-camp victims) to another ten months of suffering.

This history raises serious questions about Hannah Arendt's thesis of totalitarianism. The gist of her argument is twofold: first, that totalitarian systems such as Nazism and Communism are in their essence more similar than different since they operate on the same dynamic of appealing to isolated, anomic individuals, and use the same strategy, that of terror, in controlling populations; and second, that they are indeed total, overwhelming in their control over society and its masses, so that their domination is virtually unshakable. It is true that she says totalitarian domination contains the seeds of its own destruction, and that "every end in history necessarily contains a new beginning,"[46] but this rhetoric is not otherwise supported in her work.

Fascism is, to the contrary, significantly different in its dynamic from Communism. It constitutes a continuation of capitalism in another form, and even in its later catastrophic stage does not fundamentally challenge the principle of private ownership and private profit. It changes the form of the accumulation of capital to some degree (utilizing the looting of conquered peoples to supplement domestic exploitation) but the state and private industry continue to work hand in glove, even though imperfectly and sometimes (but not inevitably or in every case) to the detriment of industry. It requires expansion in order to survive.

Communism by contrast constitutes a revolutionary break with capitalism. Even though it leads to the domination of a new class, it is not a class based on private ownership. Expansion is not inherent in its economic structure. (See the next chapter.) Both fascism and Communism use the instruments of terror against specific populations seen as deviant or unreliable, but Communism, though it occasionally manipulates racist and anti-Semitic sentiment, is not inherently racist. Fascism comes out of a reaction against the ills of modernity. It is inherently nationalistic and expansionist, and logically racist; Communism is a distorted component of modernity, and speaks the language of the Enlightenment.

Neither fascism nor Communism is as totalitarian as in Arendt's model. Resistance and rebellion took place in both systems. In the former it ultimately failed, but we will not know whether in sufficient time it might have succeeded. Thankfully, fascism's defeat in the war preempted that possibility. But resistance under Communism succeeded after many years.

The idea that fascism comes to power when the bourgeoisie is no longer capable of ruling *through a parliamentary state* needs to be understood very precisely. The parliamentary state implies the participation of political parties that provide legitimation for the dominant social class. It therefore runs the risk that some of these parties will act against that class, and will demand too much in the way of reform. The dominant class must then decide between a risky legitimacy and a stable autocracy without legitimacy. But such a stability is precarious, as can be seen in Third World countries, because the mass of the population is excluded from the political process and is economically exploited as well. Rebellion is inevitable. In the case of fascism, a semblance of legitimacy can be provided by the movement, obviously a preferred therapy for a capitalist class mired in economic crisis. Only later do some elements of capital learn that the cure is worse than the disease.

## NOTES

1. Karl Marx, "The Eighteenth Brumaire of Louis Bonaparte," in Karl Marx and Friedrich Engels, *Selected Works*, vol. 1 (1852; reprint, London: Lawrence & Wishart, 1950), 302.

2. Ernest Mandel, introduction to Leon Trotsky, *The Struggle Against Fascism in Germany* (New York: Pathfinder Press, 1970), 10.

3. Pierre Ayçoberry, *The Nazi Question* (New York: Pantheon Books, 1981), contains a very thorough review of all the major interpretations. See also the bibliographical essay in Michael N. Dobkowski and Isidor Wallimann, eds., *Radical Perspectives on the Rise of Fascism in Germany, 1919–1945* (New York: Monthly Review Press, 1989).

4. David Schoenbaum, *Hitler's Social Revolution* (Garden City, N.Y.: Doubleday, Anchor, 1967), xxi–xxii.

5. Hermann Rauschning, *The Revolution of Nihilism* (New York: Alliance Book Corp., 1939); Jose Ortega y Gasset, *The Revolt of the Masses* (New York: W. W. Norton, 1932, 1957); Hadley Cantril, *The Psychology of Social Movements* (New York: John Wiley & Sons, 1941), 256.

6. Trotsky, *The Struggle Against Fascism in Germany*, 402.

7. Richard Hamilton, *Who Voted for Hitler?* (Princeton, N.J.: Princeton University Press, 1982), 421.

8. Hannah Arendt, *The Origins of Totalitarianism* (New York: World Publishing, 1966), 317.

9. Erich Fromm, *Escape from Freedom* (New York: Avon Books, Discus, 1965).

10. Ortega y Gasset, *The Revolt of the Masses*, 38, 84–85.

11. Franz Neumann, *Behemoth* (New York, Harper & Row, 1966), 367.

12. Fromm, *Escape from Freedom*, 232.

13. Ibid., p. 163.

14. T. W. Adorno et al., *The Authoritarian Personality* (New York: Harper & Row, 1950).

15. Gordon W. Allport, *The Nature of Prejudice* (Garden City, N.Y.: Doubleday, Anchor, 1958). Chapter 26 deals with demagogy. According to Allport, the prejudiced personality is closely related to the authoritarian personality. (See chaps. 5 and 26.)

16. Wilhelm Reich, *The Mass Psychology of Fascism* (New York: Orgone

Institute Press, 1946), ix.

17. Ibid., 301.

18. Alfredo Rocco, *The Political Doctrine of Fascism* (New York: Carnegie Endowment for International Peace, 1926), 10.

19. Ibid., 25, 12.

20. Jackson Lears, *No Place of Grace* (New York: Pantheon Books, 1981), 309. Lears's work is a comprehensive study of the history of antimodernity and its many branches. Although primarily focusing on U.S. culture from 1880–1920, there is a useful section on Europe, from which this quotation is drawn.

21. Seymour Martin Lipset, *Political Man* (1959; reprint, Baltimore, Md.: Johns Hopkins Press, 1981), 148.

22. Ibid., p. 144.

23. Brian Peterson, "Regional Elites and the Rise of National Socialism, 1920–33," in *Radical Perspectives on the Rise of Fascism in Germany, 1919–1945*, ed Michael N. Dobkowski and Isidor Walliman (New York: Monthly Review Press, 1989), 172.

24. See, for example, William S. Allen, *The Nazi Seizure of Power: The Experience of a Single German Town 1930–1935* (Chicago: University of Chicago Press, 1965). In the present author's birthplace, a stable and predominantly Catholic town, the Nazi vote increased from 3.8 percent in 1924 to 31.3 percent in 1932 (*Soester Zeitschrift* 104 [1992]).

25. Daniel Lerner, *The Nazi Elite* (Stanford, Calif.: Stanford University Press, 1951), 84.

26. Schoenbaum, *Hitler's Social Revolution*, 285.

27. R. Palme Dutt, *Fascism and Social Revolution* (New York: International Publishers, 1934), 88.

28. Robert A. Brady, *The Spirit and Structure of German Fascism* (New York: Viking Press, 1937), 22.

29. See Ayçoberry, esp. chaps. 4 and 9.

30. Trotsky, *The Struggle Against Fascism in Germany*, 407.

31. Ibid., 155.

32. Ibid., 402.

33. Kurt Gossweiler, "Economy and Politics in the Destruction of the Weimer Republic," in Dobkowski and Walliman, *Radical Perspectives on the Rise of Fascism*, 158.

34. Ibid., p. 163.

35. Ibid., p. 167.

36. David Abraham, *The Collapse of the Weimer Republic* (Princeton: Princeton University Press, 1981), 315, 320.

37. Konrad Heiden, *Der Fuehrer* (Boston: Houghton Mifflin, 1944), 264.

38. Henry A. Turner, *German Big Business and the Rise of Hitler* (New York: Oxford University Press, 1985).

39. Gossweiler, in Dobkowski and Walliman, *Radical Perspectives on the Rise of Fascism*, 167.

40. Neumann, *Behemoth*, 288–92.

41. Nicos Poulantzas, *Fascism and Dictatorship* (London: New Left Books, 1974).

42. Jane Caplan, "Theories of Fascism: Nicos Poulantzas as Historian," in Dobkowski and Walliman, *Radical Perspectives on the Rise of Fascism*, 141.

43. Ibid., 137.

44. Also see Ayçoberry, *The Nazi Question*, 208–15.

45. Ibid., p. 145.

46. Arendt, *The Origins of Totalitarianism*, 478.

# 6

# THE STATE AND
# COMMUNISM

Nineteen eighty-nine looked to be the best of years. The end of
the cold war in Europe, the likely elimination of the threat of
nuclear destruction, and the downfall of Stalinist dictatorships, all
cause for a universal sigh of relief. The convergence of military
stand-down with political liberalization in the East seemed, at the
time, to open up vast new opportunities for political democracy, and
to create space for the development of truly parliamentary governments in the image of bourgeois democracy. Western socialists
shared this optimism, for many of them thought that now that the
repressive regime of "statist socialism" was gone, there would be
room for real, democratic socialism to emerge as a viable force.

But this perspective was quickly shown to be deeply flawed, and
the events of the recent past have turned most of those hopes to
ashes. The voters of Leningrad began the new era by restoring the
name St. Petersburg. Romanian and Croatian oppositionists con-
versed with exiled kings. Tito's relatively benign regime collapsed
into civil war. Nuclear weaponry became a black market item and,
very quickly, an international market for surplus weapons systems
provided arms to a dozen local wars (some two dozen countries are
at war currently).

"Bourgeois" critics of socialism boasted of the triumph of capitalism even as emiseration began to dominate the daily existences of millions of the citizens of the former "real existing socialism." Marxism as a "Weltanschauung" was relegated by "scholars" to the dustbin of graduate student theses, and, right on schedule, a few more former socialist intellectuals appeared on the mastheads of neoconservative magazines, harkening once again to the trumpets of opportunity.

The downfall of the bureaucratic dictatorships of Eastern Europe has led in only one or two cases to stable bourgeois republics (excluding the annexation of East Germany to the Federal Republic), although the trappings of parliamentarianism are widespread. There are no signs anywhere of political power for the working class. Instead, there are poverty, racketeering, ethnic and national conflict, and civil war. Poverty and racketeering are rationalized as the normal working of neoliberal "free market" capitalism, a necessary phase in the development of true capitalism, while ethnic conflicts are attributed to primordial tribal disputes. Grotesque clamorings for the benefits of free enterprise (hence the deficits of emiseration) are paired with virtual warlord conditions of government in many places, under the ironic Leninist and Wilsonian rubric of "self-determination" coupled to the Hitlerian vocabulary of "ethnic cleansing."

The collapse of the Stalinist (or, as some would prefer, "real existing socialist") system came as a shock to many analysts. Neither social democrats nor revolutionary socialists had ever shared the assumptions of either the Communist parties or of conventional political scientists, namely that the political structures of Stalinist societies were immutable, hence unalterable without external intervention. The anti-Stalinist Left can stand on its record of denying that immutability, despite the attempts of media pundits and pseudo-intellectuals to smear the entire Left for the failings of "Communism." Nevertheless, even the Left was unprepared for the speed and depth of the changes that followed Glasnost, and even less for the astounding rate of collapse of Soviet-style regimes after May 1989, when Hungary dismantled its border with Austria, setting off the massive exodus of East Germans to West Germany that led to the opening of the Berlin Wall. "Experts" on the cold war, on Soviet society, and on totalitarianism more generally, from Hannah Arendt and relatively benign "Real-politik" analysts such as George Kennan, to hard-line cold-war interventionists like John Foster Dulles, and even more recent writers, from liberals such as Agnes Heller to conservatives like Jeanne Kirkpatrick, had all misjudged the dynamics of Soviet society. But the democratic Left found itself only slightly less wanting with respect to explanations.

Two assumptions about the way Eastern European statist regimes would undergo change were widely shared by both conventional social scientists and democratic socialists. One was that change would be fiercely resisted by all Stalinist regimes, as was the case in China and, early on, Romania, because in theory no set of rulers, especially one as well-organized and repressive as the Soviet regime, voluntarily abdicates. Cold warriors had been divided about strategy: containment (for an indefinite time) versus "roll-back" (intervention). Socialists had theorized that militant working classes would eventually be the key element in the overthrow of these repressive systems, combining tactics of general strike with armed insurrection on the model of the Hungarian Revolution of 1956. Hence there would be true revolutions from below. Left theory assumed that the downfall of the old regime would most likely bring the organized working class to political, hence to economic, power, and that working-class structures, possibly in the form of true soviets, would destoy the old, and become the new, state.

All of these assumptions were pretty far off. Containment would not last for eternity. Nor would the Stalinist regimes be overthrown by interventionist or "white" forces. As for Left theories, it is true that mass uprisings were the key to the overthrow of the Eastern European dictatorships. But most of these regimes surrendered rather quickly, some almost gracefully. The internal problems of Soviet-style societies were far more severe, their police apparatus far weaker, than most observers had anticipated. It soon became clear that the Soviet Union's military would not intervene against mass uprisings outside Russia. Its ruling class was more fractured than many had thought. Multiclass, multitendencied popular movements in which the working class (with a few exceptions) played only a secondary role took the field under the flag of democratic change but lacking any program for economic restructuring, at least at first. Groups advocating "real" socialism, or a third, Swedish-style way, were rapidly dispersed by political "reform-if-you-would-preserve" approaches that coupled parliamentary democratization (sometimes more apparent than real) to an advocacy of galloping privatization. The German Democratic Republic (GDR) was annexed to West Germany and German capital against only minimal and impotent protest. Communist parties shed themselves of their more embarrassing hard-line comrades, changed their names, and reorganized in desperate attempts to stay on top of the situation. Almost everywhere, the heirs of the revolutions against the Stalinist state have been elites, including elements of the old Communist ruling hierarchy.

The working classes in these societies had been systematically depoliticized, that is, alienated from the political process, over the years. They proved incapable of playing a leading role, or when they did, as in the Polish Solidarity movement, were fairly soon shunted aside with their leadership coopted. In any case large segments rejected any program with the discredited term "socialism" in it. If there has been a revolution (meaning: that a different class now dominates the economic and political institutions) it has not been to the benefit of the "toiling masses," the workers and the peasantry. They have little if any more social power than before; older workers in, say, the GDR, might argue they have less.

The old ruling class of bureaucrats has been displaced as a class, even as its individual members have somehow managed to find niches in the new order of affairs. Yet to consider the new order a bourgeois one would surely be a distortion. The present bourgeoisie of the

Soviet Union is hardly in the image of the hardy burghers who fought the ancien regimes of France or Britain, or even the solid citizens who, with Calvinist or Confucian logic saved, invested, profited, and reinvested in order to create modern, rational, and, at least in their ideals, republican regimes (although slavery was hardly compatible with the slogan of liberty, equality, fraternity). It is more as if the Mafia were synonymous with capitalism, which it may be on occasion, but not as a general rule.

If the old order has collapsed, and the working class has not attained power, who are the present rulers of the former statist societies? That is, what is their class nature, these former "socialist" bureaucrats wedded to "free markets"? This is the new version of the "Russian Question" that so concerned the Left for more than three-quarters of a century. But the new version of the question cannot be addressed coherently until we are clear on the old one, on what the Soviet system was, because that system was the womb out of which the present, with all its failings, has issued.

Conventional social science had little to tell us about the relationship between class and state in the former Soviet Union, primarily because "class" is usually confused with "stratum," and because the idea that states are class instruments is a (figuratively and literally) foreign one, that is, it is correctly perceived to be associated with the subversive social science of Karl Marx. It is not that the sociology of Soviet society has been totally useless, since a number of observers have been quite acute in dissecting the economic and political layers of the USSR. Much of this work has been what might be called sophisticated Kremlinology, that is, analysis of Soviet elites. Some came closer to the Marxian theories to be discussed below in that they were concerned with the issue of stability and change (not surprising, since some of this research was funded by the U.S. government, including intelligence agencies, during the cold war).

In 1950, for example, sociologist Alex Inkeles (who was involved in government research) presented the following prognosis:

The present system of stratification seems to be not merely stable, but is of such an order that it would probably require a new social and political revolution to restore the kind of dynamism necessary to create even an approximation of a classless society as defined in classical Marxist terms.... The reasons for this inhere in the very structure of contemporary Soviet society. For the social classes which are currently most highly rewarded in income, status, and power are precisely those social groups on which the present regime relies most heavily as its basis of social support. A new program aimed at social equality could, therefore, be accomplished only at the expense, hence with the alienation, of those groups on whose support the regime rests.[1]

Translating this into Marxian terms, what was Inkeles saying? Simply put, the class that benefits from a particular kind of state is unlikely to overthrow it. But it will turn out, some forty years later, that this does not mean the system is stable after all, nor that some fractions of the ruling class will not chafe at the bit and seek change.

A similarly pessimistic view about the likelihood of change is based on the idea that the Soviet Union is totalitarian, and totalitarian societies by definition root out all potential opposition. This view is often associated with the work of Hannah Arendt that was discussed in the previous chapter. Nazism and Stalinism both are totalitarian, both are dictatorships that result from the isolation and atomization of the individual in mass society, both deliberately destroy (or absorb) all organizations that could act to give identity and power to individuals—the organizations involved in what is today termed "civil society." Totalitarian states can therefore presumably be overthrown only by external armed force (as the Nazis were: this was the ultimate argument of the "roll-back" faction of the cold warriors).

For serious analysis of the class nature of the Soviet state we must turn elsewhere, to the Left. Leftist views of Soviet-style societies have traditionally fallen into three broad categories, with numerous (almost infinite) variations on each, and, at least outside the Soviet bloc, with each variation identified with a Left party or sect. One of these categories of analysis is now demonstrably bankrupt, and the others require serious amendment. Still, one of them at least grasped the basic dynamic of the nature of Soviet class society and its relationship to the Soviet state.

Probably the most widely accepted analysis (associated with the terms "socialist countries" and "real-existing socialism") was that of the old Communist Parties: The Soviet Union was a workers' state. Capitalist ideologues eagerly assented to this identification of socialism with such disparate countries as Russia, the People's Republic of China, Cuba, and Albania. Current mainstream media boasts, that the collapse of Eastern European "Communism" demonstrates the bankruptcy of socialism, are only the latest version of more than three-quarters of a century of using every failing within the bloc as a cudgel to discredit all socialist ideas. These efforts have, on balance, been fairly successful.

Although it is surely true that recent events have demonstrated once and for all that these "workers' states" did not represent the working class, failed to deliver on many of their material promises, and were opposed by many sectors of the "popular masses" that in Communist analysis supposedly gave them loyalty, such illusions had been rejected by the non-Communist Left decades ago.

Orthodox Trotskyism has regarded the Soviet system as a degenerated or deformed workers' state, its ruling clique constituting a short-term formation analogous to Bonapartism that would, in the absence of a workers' uprising, return the country to capitalism. Was Trotsky, then, right after all, and just premature? So far we have seen neither a workers' uprising (though there have been large-scale mobilizations and strikes) nor a full-scale turn to capitalism as it is ordinarily understood. A smooth transition was excluded for the simple reason that Stalinist society lacked even the most rudimentary institutions of private capital accumulation. However, the idea that Communist bureaucracies (perhaps in collaboration with non-Communist Parties) might some day perform the Bonapartist function of carving out a path to a capitalist mode of production and capitalist social relations is no longer so fanciful, even if that path was hardly the one envisioned by Trotsky.

The Trotskyist prediction was that "either the bureaucracy, becoming ever more the organ of the world bourgeoisie in the workers' state, will overthrow the new forms of property [nationalized property] and plunge the country back to capitalism; or the working class will crush the bureaucracy and open the way to socialism."[2] Trotsky's timing (he predicted that the outcome would be clear immediately after World War II) was off, no minor problem when we are talking about a half-century, but his more serious error was the prediction that the working class would militantly defend the gains of the October Revolution in the form of socialized or nationalized property against every effort by the "Bonapartist" bureaucracy to privatize it. That error was linked to the problem of timing, for by Gorbachev's time, Trotsky's working class, historically and personally linked to the 1917 Revolution, no longer existed. And the "Bonapartists" had made no effort to privatize anything for a generation and more; quite the contrary.

The third Marxist method of analysis, the "new class" concept, associated with "neo-Trotskyism" and later with Milovan Djilas, is also called into question by recent events. If the bureaucracies of Eastern Europe constituted a ruling class (by virtue of their command over the states that owned and controlled the nationalized economies of those countries), why did they not exert their class power in military form in order to protect their privileges, as in China, or as in the past? After all, if the fundamental configuration of dialectically opposed class forces consists of the new class of bureaucrats versus the working class, then a revolution in the proper sense should have pitted the working class against the bureaucracy. For neo-Trotskyists and other new-class theorists as well as for more orthodox Trotskyists the problem is the absence of the working class as a major actor in the events of the past few years, again with a few exceptions.

If Trotsky had been right, the failure of the working class immediately after World War II to "crush" the Stalinist bureaucracy should then have led to Western capitalism's successful overthrow of the remnants of the October Revolution with the full support of the "Bonapartist" bureaucrats, who should have been holding the door open. Instead, the Soviet Union quickly extended its rule westward to the Elbe, and south to the Yugoslav and Greek borders, eradicating almost all vestiges of capitalism, large or small, that might have become the germs of bourgeois restoration. The regime held tightly to its reins, even after Stalin's death, and no private-owning bourgeoisie whatever existed when the system finally cracked, aside from some small-scale farming and very small business in some countries of the bloc, and some marginal and black-market retailing.

New-class theory viewed the Stalinist elite as a new form of ruling class, and therefore rejected the likelihood of capitalist restoration. The new class would reproduce itself, and only a far-reaching social revolution would suffice to overthrow it. The error was to assume that the *fundamental* class contradiction would be the *operant* contradiction, the tinder and spark for change. This was far too simplistic an approach. It turned out that the contradiction that new-class theorists anticipated, on the basis of which it was predicted that the working class would be the main revolutionary actor, turned out to be of secondary importance. A more sophisticated analysis of the class fractions of the Soviet bureaucracy, and the changing nature of productive forces (the economy), might have shed a more accurate light on the *secondary* factors that ultimately proved so critical.

On the other hand, new-class theory was much better able to predict, or at least account for, the switches and turns of Soviet (and Chinese Communist) policy over the years, and above all to explain the longevity of these dictatorships, than other theories. Indeed, only new-class theory can account for the new regimes' difficulties in "restoring" capitalism on a structure that had utterly shattered the bourgeoisie.

New-class theory in its neo-Trotskyist form was shaped in the course of a battle within Trotskyism that came about in response to the Russo-Finnish wars. In August 1939, Stalin and Hitler signed a nonaggression pact and divided Poland between them, signaling the beginning of World War II. In November, Stalin went to war against Finland, ostensibly to prevent Finland from becoming a launching pad for an imperialist attack on the Soviet Union. As Soviet and Finnish troops hammered each other in the bitter cold of that winter, the Trotskyist movement abroad confronted its own battle: what position should be taken on the war, and specifically, should the Soviet Union be defended? Trotsky supported the Soviet Union in its defense against imperialism viewing it as a "degenerated" workers' state, but a workers' state nevertheless; the dissenters in his movement took a stance that was, in effect, neutral in the war between two similarly imperialistic and class-ruled societies.

There were two Russo-Finnish wars: The "Winter War" of 1939–40, and the "Continuation War" of 1941–44. Finland had joined Germany when the latter attacked the Soviet Union in 1941. By that time, Trotsky was dead, the victim of an assassin sent by the Soviet secret police. His followers continued to defend the Soviet Union.

As early as 1938, however, some members of the American Trotskyist party, the Socialist Workers Party, had already been moving toward a position that rejected the notion that the Soviet Union was any sort of workers' state, arguing that the Stalin bureaucracy was actually counterrevolutionary because the proletariat no longer had any say in running "its" state. In April 1940, the Trotskyists split, with a faction that included this earlier group, plus others, forming a new group called the Workers Party. This group was led by a man who had been a close ally of Trotsky, Max Shachtman, and included, among many others, James Burnham, who would later write a well-known conservative tract, *The Managerial Revolution*.[3] In June 1941, the Nazis invaded the Soviet Union. Although some in the Workers Party felt that the Soviet Union constituted a lesser evil to Nazi Germany, Shachtman and the majority of his group closed ranks against any defense of the Soviet Union and, after the United States entered the war that December, against any support for this "imperialist war." The Shachtmanite point of view appeared superficially to be a revision of orthodox Marxism because in classical Marxist theory bureaucracies could not be anything but structures dependent upon a class base rooted in some form of property ownership. In the capitalist epoch, all state forms, whether parliamentary, authoritarian, or even fascist, were ultimately determined by capitalist property and class relations. So if in the Soviet Union the 1917 Revolution (and even more so Stalin's First Five-Year Plan) had eradicated private property, and all capital was "collectivized" under the ownership of the state, then it followed that the only possible alternative to a capitalist state was a workers' state since that was the only class in existence (now that the private land-holding peasantry had been liquidated). If it was not capitalist, it must be socialist.

Trotsky put it this way:

> The character of the social regime is determined first of all by the property relations. The nationalization of the land, of the means of production and exchange, with the monopoly of foreign trade in the hands of the state, constitutes the bases of the social order of the USSR. ... By these property relations, lying at the basis of class relations, is determined for us the nature of the Soviet Union as a proletarian state.[4]

But Shachtman refused to be bound by the old either-or alternative. At the same time he did not relinquish the Marxist definition of class. While accepting Trotsky's description of the facts, he came to a different conclusion. In Russia:

> The state expropriates the private owners of land and capital, and ownership of land, and the means of production and exchange, becomes vested in the *state*...its social power lies in its political power...in the proletarian state they are inseparable.... In the

Soviet Union the proletarian is master of property only if he is master of the State which is its repository ... (therefore the) political expropriation of the proletariat ... is nothing more or less than the destruction of the class rule of the workers, the end of the Soviet Union as a workers' state. ... The *qualitative* difference lies precisely in this: the bureaucracy is no longer the controlled and revocable ... employed by the workers' state ... but the owners and controllers of the state.[5]

In a nutshell, when the state controls the economy, social power lies in political power; and if the workers have no political power, they have no social power. It is the bureaucratic dictatorship that has political power, hence social power. That is what makes it a ruling class.

For Trotsky on the other hand, nationalized property implies a workers' state, and it had to be defended. The Stalin clique was "centrist," vacillating between bourgeois tendencies (the New Economic Policy, Bukharin, the old Bolshevik Right), and proletarian tendencies (Trotsky, the Left Opposition), caught in a host of "inner contradictions" that must be resolved following the end of World War II. If a successful revolution against the bureaucracy did not follow on the heels of the war, "Imperialism will sweep away the regime which issued from the October revolution ... the inner contradictions of the Soviet Union not only might, but must, lead to a bourgeois Bonapartist counterrevolution ... without the interference of revolution, the social bases of the Soviet Union must be crushed."[6]

But Trotsky left open a back door:

Degeneration [of the workers' state] must inescapably end at a certain state in downfall. ... If contrary to all probabilities the October Revolution fails during the course of the present war, or immediately thereafter, to find its continuation in any of the advanced countries; and if, on the contrary, the proletariat is thrown back everywhere ... then we should doubtlessly have to pose the question of revising our conception of the present epoch and its driving forces. In that case it would be a question not of slapping a copybook label on the USSR or the Stalinist gang but of re-evaluating the world historical perspective.... Have we entered the epoch of social revolution and socialist society, or on the contrary the epoch of the declining society of totalitarian bureaucracy?[7]

Trotsky did not live to engage in that reevaluation. He was assassinated in Mexico by an agent of Stalin on August 20, 1940.

It would be an understatement to say that people on the Left were less than interested in the precise nature of Soviet society during World War II. Moreover, the Workers Party's antiwar position was distinctly in the minority within the broader Left, the vast majority of which supported the war effort. Irving Howe's verdict that "Trotsky's stand on the war had not the slightest practical consequence" could as well be extended not only to the Shachtmanites, but to the entire antiwar Left, such as it was.[8]

The neo-Trotskyists, given their Marxist-based conception of the class nature of the Soviet state, believed that Stalinism arose not out of the evil intent of Lenin or Stalin, or for that matter inevitably from the theories of Marx, but out of the exigencies of the particular history of Russia. In broad outline, their argument was that in a relatively backward country saddled with an antiquated nobility and handicapped by a weak bourgeoisie, a revolution had been made and carried through by the working class, some of the peasantry, and elements of the armed forces. The young Soviet state, surrounded by hostile forces, suffered immense losses in the period of war (against outside imperialist armies and counterrevolutionary or "white" forces) that followed the 1917 Revolution. The consequence was that the proletariat, its leadership decimated by war, was too weak to create a workers' state and maintain it on its own behalf. With the collapse and defeat of revolutionary forces in the more advanced countries of Western Europe, Russia was forced to rely on its own internal resources, that is, to industrialize rapidly without foreign assistance. In short, the Soviet regime was forced to exploit its own population. The almost inevitable result was the development, over the course of the 1920s, of a bureaucratic and eventually dictatorial state. Although there has been some argument as to the degree of inevitability of this development,[9] there is widespread agreement that the obstacles to the maintenance of a democratic workers' soviet state were immense. Neo-Trotskyism came to the conclusion that the development of a new ruling class under Stalin was "overdetermined" by these obstacles, thus was virtually inevitable once the revolution in the West was crushed. Indeed, Lenin and Trotsky had both been pretty pessimistic about the outcome of the October Revolution given these obstacles. Trotsky argued that Stalin's motto "socialism in one country" was an illusion in the case of a backward country such as Russia; in the absence of a second workers' revolution, bourgeois restoration was inevitable, he thought.

The dynamics of the failure of socialist revolutions had been analyzed and even predicted in certain circles earlier on, not only at the very beginnings of the Russian Revolution, but even long before it. As early as 1896 the political theorist Gaetano Mosca had proposed that "even in societies organized (on collectivist lines) there would still be those who would manage the public wealth and then the great mass who are managed."[10] Another observer, Robert Michels, whose topic of investigation was the old German Social Democratic Party, wrote in 1911 that regardless of ideological ends, organizational means would lead to oligarchy: "It is organization which gives birth to the domination of the elected over the electors, of the mandatories over the mandators, of the delegates over the delegators. Who says organization, says oligarchy."[11] He posited that, "The administration of an immeasurably large capital, above all when this capital is collective property, confers upon the administrator influence at least equal to that possessed by the private owners of capital.... The socialists might conquer, but not socialism, which would perish in the moment of its adherents' triumph."[12]

Michels did not believe that any organization, even an anarchist one, could remain free from the "iron law of oligarchy," as it came to be known. Taking a page from the work of the German sociologist

Max Weber, "iron lawyers" such as sociologist and ex-Shachtmanite Philip Selznick took it for granted that there will be bureaucracies, hence there will be oligarchy.[13] The liberal belief in the possibility of a balance of power that might offset this tendency, a view promoted by sociologist and also a former follower of Max Shachtman, Seymour Martin Lipset, was seen as illusory. Logically, the only way to prevent the iron law from working was to stop history, the politics of consistent conservatism, the road that would be taken by James Burnham.

Even among the old Bolsheviks there had been some awareness of this general approach. The very last two pages of Nikolai Bukharin's *Historical Materialism* in fact takes up Michels's challenge specifically, only to dismiss it: in communist society "the fundamental basis for the formation of monopoly groups will disappear…there will be a colossal overproduction of organizers, which will nullify the *stability* of the ruling groups."[14] Shachtman also took note of this years later, but only in order to use one phrase, where Bukharin says that in the transition to socialism, in the period of the dictatorship of the proletariat, the "leading stratum" may exhibit the characteristics of a "class-germ," meaning, in Shachtman's eyes, the seeds of a new class.[15]

Anarchists too had warned of the dangers of oligarchy inherent in socialism and communism. It was not organization or bureaucracy as such that disturbed anarchists, as it did the "iron lawyers." Rather, it was the state, any state, regardless of its class content. For anarchists, government inevitably creates oligarchies. Bakunin, Kropotkin, and others all agreed that the privileges and hierarchies inevitably involved in all governments would always "under the pretense of making men moral and civilising them," enslave, oppress, exploit, and ruin them.[16]

In the revolutionary socialist movement, the most important foreshadowing of new-class theory was in the writings of Rosa Luxemburg. Her pamphlet *The Russian Revolution*, written from a German prison cell in 1918 shortly before her murder, apparently did not appear in the United States until 1940. Her prophetic words are well worth repeating:

Public control is indispensably necessary. Otherwise the exchange of experiences remains only within the closed circle of the officials of the new regime. Corruption becomes inevitable.... In place of the representative bodies created by general popular elections, Lenin and Trotsky have laid down the soviets as the only true representation of the laboring masses. But with the repression of political life in the land as a whole, life in the soviets must also become more and more crippled. Without general elections, without a free struggle of opinion, life dies out in every public institution, becomes a mere semblance of life, in which only the bureaucracy remains as the active element. Public life gradually falls asleep, a few dozen party leaders of inexhaustible energy and boundless experience direct and rule. Among them, in reality only a dozen outstanding heads do the leading and an elite of the working class is invited from time to time to meetings where they are to applaud the speeches of the leaders, and to approve proposed resolutions unanimously—at bottom, then, a clique affair— a dictatorship, to be sure, not the dictatorship of the proletariat, however, but only the dictatorship of a handful of politicians.... Yes, we can go even further: such conditions must inevitably cause a brutalization of public life: attempted assassinations, shootings of hostages, etc.[17]

According to Anton Ciliga, who spent some time in a Soviet prison, the next revolutionaries who would submit Lenin to such a critique were the Workers Group, the extreme wing of the Workers Opposition in Russia. As early as 1922 this group "considered that the alleged socialism which was being constructed under compulsion was actually bureaucratic state capitalism."[18] Ciliga's book *The Russian Enigma* appeared in Paris in 1938, and a year later another book, *La Bureaucratisation du Monde*, by one "Bruno R." (Rizzi), further promoted the idea that there was a third alternative to both capitalism and socialism, what Rizzi called "bureaucratic collectivism." Rizzi's views anticipated those of James Burnham, with a different twist: Rizzi *favored* the development of rational, planned states, including the New Deal, Stalinism, and Mussolini's fascism, as an alternative to capitalism.[19]

After the war, the debate about the likely future of class rule not only in Soviet society but also in the West continued in the by-now miniscule anti-Stalinist Left, and extended out from it as numerous socialists ran down the red flag and moved, some gradually and others more rapidly, rightward. James Burnham, one of Shachtman's comrades in the split with Trotsky, resigned from the Workers Party almost immediately after its formation, having taken the theory of the new class, by then formally termed "bureaucratic collectivism," to what he considered its logical conclusion. In his letter of resignation dated May 21, 1940, he said:

> Not only do I believe it meaningless to say that "socialism is inevitable" and false that socialism is "the only alternative to capitalism"; I consider that on the basis of the evidence now available to us a new form of exploitation (what I call "managerial society") is not only possible as an alterative to capitalism but is a more probable outcome of the present period than socialism.[20]

He then wrote *The Managerial Revolution*, in which he argued that,

> The economic framework in which this social dominance of the managers will be assured is based upon the state ownership of the major instruments of production...the state...will...be the "property" of the managers. And that will be quite enough to place them in the position of the ruling class.[21]

Burnham went farther than Shachtman in one striking respect. Burnham's position was that managerial society was not restricted to Russia. Fascist Germany and the New Deal, he said, also represented advanced stages of managerial society. This was a position quite close to the idea of "friendly fascism."

Another ex-Trotskyist, Dwight Macdonald, had meanwhile also struck out on his own, and in the midst of the war organized an antiwar "libertarian" magazine called *Politics*. In a series entitled "The Root Is Man," Macdonald wrote that, "A form of society has come into being which is not Socialism but rather an even more oppressive form of class society than Capitalism and yet which has resolved those economic contradictions on which Marx based his expectations of progress to socialism. It is a 'third alternative' to both capitalism and socialism."[22] Like Burnham, Macdonald also threw Keynsian economic policies and the postwar nationalization trend in Labor Britain into the statist pot. But he did not follow Burnham into the conservative camp. He continued to hold out hope for an alternative, left-libertarian vision.

But Burnham and Macdonald were wrong. Keynsian economic policies, some would say, were never actually put into practice except in the form of "military Keynsianism" (war-related expenditures by the capitalist state that functioned to keep employment at high levels). The nationalization trend has been stopped in its tracks by old-fashioned capitalist "free-market" policies, underwritten by most capitalist states. State regulation is very far from synonymous with control of the economy by state bureaucrats (see chapters 3 and 4). "Economic contradictions" were not resolved, not in the West, and not even in the Soviet Union, it would turn out.

It was another decade before the new-class idea would finally emerge from the relative obscurity of left sectarian debates. In 1957 the *New York Times* and Frederick A. Praeger, publisher, discovered Milovan Djilas, a former comrade of Communist dictator Josip Broz Tito, in a Yugoslav prison. Djilas, who had had some access to more or less secret archives that included the writings of Trotsky, laid out a theory of a "new class" in terms that were virtually identical to the ideas propounded years earlier by Shachtman, who himself was not, as we have noted, the originator of the concept. First as a series in the *Times* (July 1957), then in his book *The New Class*, Djilas proclaimed that "in contemporary Communism a new owning and exploiting class is involved and not merely a temporary dictatorship and an arbitrary bureaucracy."[23] Most of those who read and reviewed *The New Class* were unaware of the earlier history of this theory. The book was treated as just another "insider" exposé of the evils of Communism.

For those of a generation later, when Stalinism, symbolized by the Berlin Wall, no longer exists, it seems irrelevant whether Trotsky, or Shachtman, or Burnham, or Macdonald were right or wrong about the class nature of the former Soviet Union. The revolutionary Left's impact on the major historic events of the latter half of the twentieth century seems virtually nil. But the verdict that "third-camp socialism" (the idea that socialists would give allegience to neither Washington nor Moscow, which Shachtman and his group, among others, had championed) was irrelevant would be superficial. "Neither Washington" implied not only a rejection of capitalism, but also of reformist social democratic movements that were in the capitalist camp in the cold war, and of their tradition of bureaucratic nationalization and technocratic planning. "Nor Moscow" implied not only a rejection of the identification of socialism with the Soviet state, but also a critique of revolutionary states such as China, Cuba, and Vietnam that were formed in the image of Stalin's Russia, or were moving in that direction, states in which the working class had very circumscribed rights at best, and in which party bureaucracies entirely, or virtually, monopolized the decision-making process over all basic issues.

The collapse of the Soviet ruling class and its clones in other Eastern European countries has confronted the peoples of the former bloc with a fundamental question as to what class, hence what kind of state, will come to rule.

But first we need to examine how the old order of bureaucratic collectivism collapsed, what class forces played what roles in that collapse, and what classes and fractions of classes now exist to contest for class power, for domination of the state in whatever form.

Post hoc attempts to grapple with the confusing events surrounding the fall of the Soviet state range from the simplistic and banal to the fairly sophisticated, but a comprehensive class-based or Marxist analysis is still lacking.

There are the gropings of old-line Communists and their naive friends: the "crisis" of "real-existing socialism" is attributable to the failings of the leadership, a theory linked to the notion that Stalin made some mistakes, committed serious errors, even crimes. The contemporary version is that the economic failings of Soviet-style societies are attributable to their leaders' overly rigid refusal to allow mass participation. A centralized command economy, in this view necessary for swift development in a backward country surrounded by enemies (a highly debatable issue within the broader Left), requires bureaucracy, which is the inevitable breeding ground for corruption and stagnation. However, these errors can be reversed by opening the door to democracy, as Gorbachev apparently sought to do. Stalinism is ultimately vindicated because the Stalin regime created the material preconditions for democratic socialism, in this view. True, the old ruling group went too far in its enthusiasm for rapid industrialization from the top, hence the crisis. But Stalinism also led to Gorbachev, who by his very existence and initial success demonstrated the system's capacity for self-reform. Unfortunately for this theory, Gorbachev failed and the system, rather than reforming itself, self-destructed altogether. One could argue that this is a temporary phase that will be reversed, absent foreign intervention, but that does not appear to fit with the evidence.

This approach begs the fundamental question of how this command economy evolved over, and against, the organs of workers' democracy in the early years of the revolution. What were the historical circumstances that "permitted" a Stalin to come to power and create this overly centralized, bureaucratized, and indeed corrupt and criminal regime? Trotskyism, neo-Trotskyism, and other Left theories posit that a fundamental change in the interests of the rulers took place. What happened was no "mistake." It was the outgrowth of the self-interest of the ruling group, regardless of the label applied to it.

But that does not explain the dramatic changes of the Gorbachev years. We might begin with the hardly innovative observation that a little bit of reform opens the door to a dynamic that leads to an unanticipated sequence of events out of the control of the initiators. Marxist-based theory tells us that under capitalism, the overthrow of a dictatorship and the creation of a parliamentary state need not disturb broader capitalist relations. Under Stalinism, however, democratization necessarily opens up the issue of the economy because politics is economics: they are totally intertwined because the state controls the economy. A democratic parliament therefore functions not as a debating society about social policies that leave economic relations largely alone, but as a debating society about the totality of social relations, including the nature of the economy. The bureaucrats who wanted only to create a more open, flexible atmosphere in order to build a more civilized, modern society (even if only for themselves and not the general population) found they had let loose a Frankenstein's monster, one that threatened to crush its creators and with them, their entire class structure.

What historical developments brought the ruling group to the point that some of its elements, not just Gorbachev, became convinced that democratic reforms were essential throughout the bloc? What forces did Gorbachev represent, and how did the ideology of reform correspond to their needs?

Two intertwined factors need examination: changes in the forces of production, and corresponding changes in the class makeup and the relationship of classes in Soviet society.

The first factor must be placed into a global context, a contention familiar to world systems and "post-Fordist" thinkers. Terry Boswell and Ralph Peters's analysis seems sensible:

A world economic divide is now taking place between high skill flexible production…and low skill mass production that is shifting to the (semi) periphery. State socialist societies are experiencing extremely difficult economic reactions to the world divide because they concentrated so heavily on mass production in the post-war period.[24]

There are turning points in economic history when "accumulation innovations to foster renewed economic growth and development" must take place if a country is to avoid stagnation and reduction to dependency status.[25] Stalinist societies are ill-equipped to undertake innovation because their production methods are not adaptive. They are classical victims of organizational Darwinism: overadapted to specific circumstances (backwardness and the need for postwar reconstruction), they are unable to adapt to changing world conditions and go bankrupt.

The Stalinist model (rapid industrialization dictated from the top) cut countries of the bloc off from access to some technology (though not from trade and other contacts), and its linkage to repression made for inefficient management. Daniel Singer argues that as "the economy became more complex and people became more educated, the system designed for illiterate *muzhiks* became clearly obsolete, and an obstacle to further development.... New generations were growing incomparably more educated and less frightened."[26] Moreover, many in these younger, educated strata had by now been exposed to the West, via television (especially in East Germany) and even limited travel.

Declining gains in productivity led to a lessening of opportunity for social advancement by the educated sectors. There was discontent among those whose opportunities did not match their qualifications. "Cleavages appeared within (the party's) leadership, between ... the *apparatchiks* and the managers," as Singer puts it, that is, between those with a vested interest in stability and privilege, and consequently a fealty to old production methods, versus those with an interest in promoting modern methods to improve productivity, methods threatening to the Stalinist old guard.

With a decline in living standards throughout the society, including the working class, segments of the ruling class began to revolt, arguing that unless reforms were instituted the system would collapse. These fractions constituted a significant pressure group against repression. Some were involved in transnational economic, political, and cultural relations: the use of terror would undermine such relations. The concentration or labor camps had by now been largely abolished, hence were not a deterrent. More people were willing to take risks, and fewer willing to punish them. Finally, the economic costs of military and police repression in a weak economy may have contributed to a reluctance on the part of the command structure to resort to sustained violence. The Chinese strategy had become unacceptable for economic, political, and cultural reasons in the Soviet Union and most of its "satellite" partners.

These issues were for the most part played out *within* the ruling circles of the society, between different fractions of the party-state apparatus, rather than *between* the elite and the masses, although the threat (and the occasional reality) of mass action in the streets, and strikes, acted to underline the crisis and further motivate reform.

The collapse of bureaucratic collectivism in its classical, relatively stable form generated a splintering of the old "new class" into a multitude of class fractions that contended (and still contend), singly and in coalitions, for state power and therefore for economic power (insofar as large sectors of the economy remained, and to a significant degree still remain state property).

There are (a) the old state administrative, party, and economic sector managers and administrators. Many in this group have simply appropriated state property and privatized it into their own hands. This group therefore overlaps and partly helps to generate (b) a new class of entrepreneurs that might be viewed as an incipient native bourgeoisie. This group includes black marketeers and other racketeers, and given the wealth that some have accumulated, overlaps with (c) a group of internationally oriented carpetbaggers, swindlers, and *compradores* whose economic interest lies in representing foreign capital and selling off public property to foreign corporations. In addition, there continues to be (d) a priviliged stratum of intellectuals and professional-technical experts, who find themselves caught between loyalty to the society as a whole, versus a concern for maintaining their own special, albeit shrinking, privileges in this rapidly shifting configuration of classes-in-formation.

The collapse of central political power has also resulted in a centrifugal splintering into national and ethnic political entities. The Stalinists who ruled these fiefdoms away from the "centre," Moscow, or for that matter Belgrade, proceeded quickly to scramble to stay on their horses in order to protect their privileges. Rapidly changing shirts and flags, they play the nationalist card, even to the point of "ethnic cleansing." The struggle for ever smaller spoils has resulted in coups, countercoups, and civil war. Self-determination increasingly translated into xenophobia.

Yugoslavia, perhaps the extreme case, split off several of its constituent republics. Slovenia and Croatia, in the north, were quickly recognized as independent nations by Germany, thus finalizing the split and opening the door to further splintering. Wars within the remnant of Serbian-controlled Yugoslavia, and between it and Croatia, and Bosnia, followed. Then came its effort to purge Kosovo of pro-independence forces, and later to "cleanse" the province of Kosovar Albanians altogether, with catastrophic consequences on an international scale.

The struggle was not by any means only one of ethnic and religious rivalries, though these were certainly manipulated by all sides. It was also about control of the country's industry and black-marketing operations. A kind of warlordism, with a mass base among many workers and peasants manipulated by ethnic and religious slogans and a history of ethnic feuding, by no means limited to Yugoslavia, suggests the ultimate in "the socialism of fools." At the same time, certainly in the former Soviet Union, there exists a real conflict between the "centre," the headquarters of the ruling group, whose fortunes in the long term require an orderly country with a safe "climate for investment," and outlying warlords whose futures in a centralized, rational bourgeois order that is presumably to come after this warlord Bonapartism are doubtful.

Meanwhile the privations of privatization creates unrest. Significant sectors of the general population in Russia and East Germany, for example, still take socialist ideals seriously, despite their distortion by the former rulers (and by the contemporary media). Many, in the light of current deprivations, look back with some longing to the past, no matter how nasty and brutish it may have been. At least people ate, had a roof over their heads, had some access to medical care (minimal as it may have been), and were secure from street crime. This unrest, too, is manipulated by ultranationalists and refocused on "outsider" groups such as Jews (as always), foreigners, "gypsies," and any other available scapegoat target.

What is the character of the new regimes that have displaced the Stalinist order? There is some variation. Some are warlord states living largely by looting their weaker neighbors. They are not yet Bonapartist since the orderliness required to create new infrastructure that would be the basis of a native capitalist class has not yet been created (or in some cases, where some existed, it has been bombed into ruins). More typical in the countries of the former Soviet bloc are "neo-Bonapartist" states where the old bureaucratic class is no longer able to maintain a monopoly over the state, yet no other class is as yet sufficiently strong to create a state in its own image and rule in its own name. The bureaucracy of the neo-Bonapartist state vacillates among concessions to one or another, or a combination, of class forces. While surrendering some privileges in the name of democracy, the bureaucracy attempts to preserve its own overall status as a ruling group. Some of its concessions stimulate the development of a national bourgeoisie. Others attract foreign capital. Still others are concessions to minority nationalities and their rulers, who in turn perform the same dance. In this context, the line between being a government official and being a private entrepreneur, or even a gangster, becomes hazy. The role of parliament is to function as a debating society among these various fractions, including some representing genuinely democratic forces. But in the absence of a consensus, parliament remains impotent, and the neo-Bonapartist dictatorship fills the vacuum.

This is a situation of flux. The conditions foreign capital

requires for investment lead to the reining-in of working-class demands. Increasing corruption at many levels undermines equitable distribution of resources, leading to protests. The democratization of the political process, imperfect as it may be, unleashes bottled-up nationalist fervor, but can also foster labor unionism. In its new position facing world markets, the state finds itself competing with other states (including in the Third World) for investment. Environmental conditions, already catastrophic, are likely to suffer more, generating some "Green" sentiment.

The long-term historic function of the neo-Bonapartist state, just as with classical Bonapartism, is as a bridge, but to what? In the absence of viable bids from other classes, the Bonapartists can survive as rulers only by virtue of their ability to manipulate the economy and juggle the political situation (sometimes by regressing into a more dictatorial mode supported rhetorically by ultranationalistic posturing). As bourgeois elements become more powerful, state bureaucrats can continue on a path to becoming part of a new capitalist class and the state can succumb to the capitalist dynamic, which implies also its global dimension. This means that the state will replicate the tasks of all states in capitalist society, representing its ruling class on the world stage. Reversion to full-scale state control by a Stalinist-style bureaucracy has been attempted (by coup) but failed and is probably excluded.

Recent developments in the former Soviet Union are tragically suggestive of what is likely to transpire in the next years. The state bureaucracy, the privatized sectors of the economy, and corrupt criminal organizations are increasingly intertwined. In an odd mirror-image of Western power structures, in which the corporate and state sectors interpenetrate each other by, among other mechanisms, interchanging personnel, the Russian power structure can now be described as a network of individuals who move between privatized industry, the new banking sector, the media, the political structures and parties, criminal-racketeering elements, the military, and even the secret police in an elaborate dance generating immense profits for a few, and misery for the majority. Such an integration of power elites, one observer has written, can lead to stabilization of sorts (partly because of growing apathy on the part of the mass of the population that feels helpless to intervene). But the power structure is not a monolith, and internal conflicts do exist. "Only real conflict makes it possible for the population to inform itself. Lacking that, what remains is an ever more dense collaboration between secret police, criminal elements, moneyed power, media, and political influence."[27]

In the People's Republic of China, the penetration of capitalism, until now less in the form of the dismantling of the state sector (as in Russia) than through large-scale foreign investment, has hardly resulted in an improvement of conditions for much of the population. Low-wage, labor-intensive state-controlled industry driving an export-based economy has been a mixed blessing. Environmental degradation is serious. Rural areas remain poor and there is large-scale migration to the cities, generating huge numbers of people living in conditions no better than those of the *favelas* or shack cities of Rio or Mexico City. But now privatization has reached China too, though democratic rights for labor have not. This combination, large-scale foreign investment, low-wage labor, and a lack of protections for workers, creates a competitive economic monster that threatens the working conditions and economic security of working people throughout the entire world.

In Russia, the choice has become, as Daniel Singer once put it, "not Sweden versus Thatcher, but Mexico versus Brazil."[28] What is the choice in China? Brazil versus Indonesia under the continuing domination of what is called a Communist Party? Is the last act of the Stalinist epoch to be a debate among the former Stalinist rulers as to the degree to which industry should be privatized, and the degree of impoverishment of workers and farmers that can be safely tolerated in the interest of maintaining a privileged minority in power?

# NOTES

1. Alex Inkeles, "Social Stratification and Mobility in the Soviet Union," in *Class, Status and Power,* ed. Reinhard Bendix and Seymour Martin Lipset (New York: Free Press, 1953).

2. Fourth International, *The Death Agony of Capitalism and the Tasks of the Fourth International* (New York: Pioneer Publishers, 1938), 47; Max Shachtman, *The Struggle for the New Course* (New York: New International, 1943), 216.

3. James Burnham, *The Managerial Revolution* (New York: John Day, 1941).

4. Max Shachtman, *The Bureaucratic Revolution* (New York: Donald Press, 1962), 38.

5. Ibid., 42–44, 46, 50.

6. Quoted by Shachtman in "Pre-War Perspectives and Post-War Realities: An Analysis of the Politics of the Fourth International," *New International* (December 1945).

7. Leon Trotsky, *In Defense of Marxism* (New York: Pioneer Publishers, 1942), 13–14.

8. Irving Howe, *Leon Trotsky* (New York: Viking Press, 1978), 184.

9. Samuel Farber, *Before Stalinism: The Rise and Fall of Soviet Democracy* (London and New York: Verso, 1990).

10. Gaetano Mosca, *The Ruling Class* (1896; reprint, New York: McGraw-Hill, 1939), 284–85.

11. Robert Michels, *Political Parties* (1911; reprint, Glencoe, Ill.: Free Press, 1949), 401.

12. Ibid., 383, 391.

13. Philip Selznick, "An Approach to a Theory of Bureaucracy," *American Sociological Review* 8 (1943). See also Hans H. Gerth and C. Wright Mills, eds., *From Max Weber* (New York: Oxford University Press, 1958), chap. 8.

14. Nikolai Bukharin, *Historical Materialism* (New York: International Publishers, 1925), 310. Bukharin was a major Bolshevik leader and theoretician until his arrest in 1937. He was a defendant in the infamous Moscow purge trials (1936–38) together with other leading Bolsheviks, and was executed.

15. Shachtman, *The Bureaucratic Revolution*, 78–79.

16. Bakunin, quoted in George Woodcock, *Anarchy or Chaos* (London: Freedom Press, 1944).

17. Luxemburg's pamphlet was translated by Bertram Wolfe, then a member of the expelled Lovestone faction of the Communist Party, and published by the Workers Age Press. It appears, together with *Leninism or Marxism?* in a 1961 edition published by the University of Michigan Press, and elsewhere. For a fuller discussion, see Stephen Eric Bronner, *Rosa Luxemburg, A Revolutionary for Our Times* (New York: Columbia University Press, 1987.)

18. Anton Ciliga, "A Talk with Lenin in Stalin's Prison," *Politics* (August 1946). Also see Farber, *Before Stalinism*.

19. Ernest E. Haberkorn and Arthur Lipow, eds., *Neither Capitalism Nor Socialism* (Amherst, N.Y.: Humanity Books, 1996), Appendix A.

20. Quoted in Trotsky, *In Defense of Marxism*, Appendix, 207.

21. Burnham, *The Managerial Revolution*, 42.

22. Dwight Macdonald, *The Root Is Man* (Alhambra, Calif.: Cunningham Press, 1953; orig. in *Politics*, April, 1946), 27.

23. Milovan Djilas, *The New Class* (New York: Frederick A. Praeger, 1957), 54.

24. Terry Boswell and Ralph Peters, "State Socialism and the Industrial Divide in the World Economy," *Critical Sociology* 17, no. 1 (Spring 1990): 5.

25. Ibid.

26. Daniel Singer, "Wither the Soviet Union?" *Monthly Review* (July–August 1989): 3.

27. Erhard Stoelting, "Die Macht der Banken und die Macht der Oeffentlichkeit, ein aufklaerender Konflikt in Russland," *Kommune* (November 1997).

28. Singer, talk at Socialist Scholars Conference, New York, 1991.

# 7
# THE STATE AND
# ITS MINORITIES

*There are no longer any countries that are ethnically homogeneous.*

*In no country do ethnic minorities share proportionally in the distribution of resources.*

*All states have "agendas" (formal or informal) regarding their minority groups.*

These three statements are the framework in which all discussion of minorities must necesssarily take place. Minorities are always disadvantaged relative to the dominant ethnic group (except of course where a minority, for example, white Anglo-Saxon Episcopalians, *is* the dominant ethnic group). It is because of that seeming perpetual disadvantage that minority ethnicities almost invariably mobilize at some point around nationalist or separatist slogans as one of their major political tendencies. These mobilizations or movements are intended to overcome what minorities regard as the biased way the society (and the state) treats them. Conversely, the dominant ethnicity perpetually resists equalization or integration to one degree or another because the integration of minorities in the economy, in the political structure, and in "society" or the aristocracy cannot be accomodated without profound alterations in the class structure, in political institutions, and in elite social institutions. Each of these involve vested interests that can at best only partially accomodate the demands, and the large-scale personal participation, of subordinate ethnic groups. Hence all states, which exist to protect such vested interests, have an ethnic agenda; all states are, as Omi and Winant put it, "racial states."[1]

The class structure in its concrete, daily form translates into the workings of the labor market and the occupational system. Disadvantage means that no subordinate minority has the same access to the set of occupations in the labor market as the dominant group. Virtually all subordinate minority groups have occupational profiles that are inferior to that of the dominant group, as measured by the income and wealth these occupations generate. Conversely, most occupational groupings, broadly defined, have unique ethnic profiles such that there is an ethnic (and gender) "picture" that varies from one occupation to the next: every ethnic, racial, gender, etc., group will be over- or underrepresented in virtually every occupational grouping, to the almost invariable disadvantage of the subordinate group (including women).

To the degree that a minority does become integrated, even if only partially, meaning that its access to resources improves, it loses some of its ethnic identity. As Steinberg says, "ethnicity has been preserved most authentically by those groups who, for one reason or another, have remained economically marginal. Even among groups that have experienced wide-scale mobility, the lower-class strata continue to function as a cultural anchor for their more affluent relatives."[2] But ethnicity is also preserved by the *dominant* group as an exclusionary mechanism. In short, discrimination based on ethnicity (including race, religion, and national background) has the function of maintaining control by the dominant class, which is also the dominant (though often not the majority) ethnic group. And to one degree or another, these exclusionary mechanisms are reinforced by the state, if only by benign neglect. The most important (although by no means the only) reason that conflict between ethnic, racial, and national minorities and their dominant ethnics (who control the state) persists is that the distribution of resources between groups remains unequal.

However, to talk in this overarching, general way about ethnic or minority relations or problems disguises the complexity of the issues. Quite distinct and qualitatively different problems should not be reduced to a false common denominator. There are vast differences in the condition of different ethnic, racial, and national minorities, rooted in specific historical and economic circumstances. Although racial minorities generally face more difficult problems than minorities that belong to the dominant racial group, there are also significant differences among and within racial groups, with the added qualification that different nations identify "racial" in quite different ways. Moreover, while a particular group may be defined in racial terms in one period (presuming some sort of biological difference), it becomes relabeled with the more dignified, neutral-sounding title "ethnic" as social, economic, and political circumstances change. Italians, the Irish, and Jews have all been labeled a different "race" in the course of U.S. history, but no longer. At another level, the term "Aryan," technically referring to a linguistic family, has been coupled with the word "race" for so long that it was, and in some political quarters still is, synonymous with "Nordic" appearance even though most Aryan-speakers are dark.

Although a minority ethnic group is not necessarily a *national* minority, all *national* minorities are by definition ethnic. A national minority differs in some cultural respect from the politically dominant nationality (language, religion, and most important a common historical identity are the major distinguishing markers). Its members are sometimes physically ("racially") distinguishable from the dominant group, but not necessarily. It has roots in an identifiable geographical area, often on the periphery of the nation, a reflection of an earlier and different configuration of political boundaries, even when many of its members are dispersed thoughout the larger nation. Its members often live in one or more "ghettos," geographical pockets of high concentrations of the group.

Most ghettos to some extent resemble colonies in that there is a range of economic institutions and classes the totality of which is ultimately dependent on, and exploited by, the dominant nation in which the ghetto exists. For national minorities, this ghetto existence is underlined by cultural and historical differences, as with the Quebecois in Canada. On the other hand, not all ghettos are national minorities because they are too widely scattered (and many members may live "integrated"), as in the case of Chinese Americans, Jews in the Diaspora, or the Turks of Germany. Their historical roots are outside the country so they have no identifiable national territory inside the host nation. African Americans, too, live in many scattered ghettos, many are integrated geographically, and their historical roots are also outside the country. But their ghettos are sufficiently large that the term "internal colony" is not without relevance.[3]

The entire contemporary world consists of nations that are multiethnic. But the "mix" varies. Historically, imperial conquests coupled with the ravages of epidemics and famine resulted in vast dislocations of many peoples even prior to the carving out of modern states and the birth of colonialism in the sixteenth and seventeenth centuries. The modern nation-state and its expansion in colonial form, with attendant wars over territory and colonies, continued this long-standing historical pattern in sharper form. Within our own century large numbers of people have been annexed, conquered, expelled, or taken by force from their historical homelands and in some cases largely or partially exterminated in the course of wars and their consequences. The expulsion and then return of Albanian Kosovars, and the subsequent fleeing of Serbs from Kosovar is only one of several recent examples. Following World War II, the redrawing of the German-Polish border resulted in the "transfer" of 9.6 million Germans from their homelands to Germany; 3.5 million more were expelled from the German-speaking Sudeten part of

Czechoslovakia. Millions of refugees have been forced from their homes due to ethnic strife in Africa in the past decade. And, in a permanent footnote to history, conquering soldiers leave behind their genetic mark. Germany today has more than 30,000 black citizens; more than 60,000 Vietnamese children and other relatives of U.S. soldiers have emigrated to the United States.

Ancient empires had always been "multiethnic," but these sprawling feudal consortia (such as the Ottoman, the Russian, the Austro-Hungarian) ultimately proved incapable of competing (in the military, among other arenas) with more efficient bourgois nations, and they collapsed. Austria-Hungary was carved up into "modern" nations and the Ottoman Empire into one semimodern nation and numerous colonies under the domination of the victors of World War I. In all probability only the 1917 Soviet revolution prevented the complete disintegration of the czarist empire, a centrifugal process that resumed with the collapse of Stalinism.

Virtually without exception, the ethnic national minorities that have found themselves incorporated into larger nations have had a problematic existence, with conflict, rebellion, and strivings for independence a constant. Nationalism and separatist agitation is not limited to the Balkans. In Western Europe there is agitation in Corsica (rooted in Genoa's ceding Corsica to France in 1768), the Basque area of Spain, the continuing Irish "troubles," and many more. There are some 7 to 12 million Sinti and Romany peoples ("gypsies") scattered throughout Europe, where they are persecuted and reviled almost everywhere. The redrawing of borders after the collapse of the Hapsburg Empire resulted in Hungarians becoming the largest minority nationality in Europe west of the former Soviet Union. Two million of Hungarian background live in Romania alone. In the eastern corner of Germany bordering on Poland and the Czech Republic there are some 60,000 Sorbs; their northern group speaks a dialect of Polish, their southern compatriots a dialect of Czech. They do not identify as Germans. In Italy, 3 million Italians use 18 non-Italian languages, including German,

Albanian, Ladino, Provençal, and a Sardinian dialect, reflecting Italy's tangled history of war, unification, and annexation. In Algeria, 7 million Berbers, nearly one-third of the population, who are Muslim but not Arabic-speaking, continue to resist the state's "arabization" policies.

Farther east, "Kurdistan" spreads through northern Iraq, Iran, southeastern Turkey, and parts of Syria and the former USSR. Some 25 million Kurds (Moslems) constitute the Middle East's fourth largest ethnic group, and the world's largest nonstate nation. One-fifth of Turkey's population consists of Kurds; two-thirds of the Turkish army, the second-largest in NATO, is virtually an occupation army in Kurdish areas. In the United States, the Navajos reside in a cluster of reserves larger than many states. Still more complex are the pan-Turkic dreams said to characterize the increasingly restive inhabitants of "Turkestan," a vast area of Turkic-speaking peoples running from Turkey through northeastern Iraq, northern Iran, northern Pakistan, a number of former Soviet republics, a corner of India, and Xinjian Province in China.

In no case is the economic and social profile of a national minority congruent with that of the dominant ethnic group. National minorities, each in its own way, perform particular economic functions in what some have called a balkanized (!) labor market. In Bulgaria, ethnic Turks are essential in farming. About 300,000 have left Bulgaria in recent years due to persecution. This emigration compounded food shortages that contributed to Bulgaria's dramatically increasing national debt for a time.

Many modern nations imposed themselves on preexisting nations and cultural entities in the period before World War I, carving preliterate and literate societies in what is called the "Third World" up into colonies. The different "tribes" incorporated into those colonies, insofar as they have not been exterminated or moved elsewhere, continue to exist in what are now nominally independent nations. However, these nations inherited their artificial boundaries from colonial days so that almost without exception newly independent former colonies suffer internal disputes rooted in the fact that minority (sometimes even majority) nations and cultures based on historical differences of a political, linguistic, religious, or economic kind find themselves within the boundaries of a nation ruled by others. In order to develop a coherent economic structure, it is necessary for these new nations to forge the kind of national identity common to "modern" society. This motivates their political leaders (often of a "Bonapartist" type) to suppress their subordinate national minorities, exacerbating internal strife. In many parts of Africa (the list is depressingly long) the struggle between older entities who now live in new, artificial homes in which one is dominant and the other subordinate, and in which each has some claim to legitimate leadership and each wishes to forge a national identity in its own image, has resulted in a score of bitter civil wars, economic collapse, famine, and deaths at genocidal levels.

In a number of instances colonial conquest resulted in the colonizers becoming more numerous than the aboriginal inhabitants. The colonizers in such nations as Canada, the United States, Australia, and in somewhat different form in many Latin American countries, and in Israel, succeeded in driving much or all of the aboriginal population off their lands and turning them into a marginal sub- or lumpenproletariat of day laborers, or driving them into the mountains to scratch out a miserable existence on marginal lands, or herding them into reserves (or refugee camps) to make their livings, at best, as anthropological or touristic curiosities. The forced flight of an entire population from its lands and its marginalization in neighboring countries or in internationally sponsored refugee camps is another version. Such subordinate groups constitute, today, the absolutely poorest populations in the world. At the same time, in at least some cases (the Palestinians are an example), the outcome has been the development of a national identity where little of that had existed earlier (during Ottoman days), and an ineradicable and burning nationalism.

These settler nations or nations of immigrants treat subsequent waves of immigrants differently, seeing some as desirable (to meet labor-market needs or maintain a racial or ethnic balance) and others as undesirable (in times of labor surplus or the perception of a threat to the dominant culture). But no matter how badly they are treated, it is never as badly as the aboriginal population. Yet the occupational profiles of later immigrant groups, no matter how desirable they are seen to be, and no matter how long they have been in the country, differ somewhat from (and are almost aways inferior to) those of the dominant earlier groups, and reflect in historically diluted form their occupational chances at the time of their arrival. Those who arrive under fortuitous circumstances and bring with them money, or talents appropriate to the labor market at the time, do better, especially if they are of the same "race" as the dominant group, and this advantageous beginning trickles down to later generations.

Some nations contain within their boundaries another nation that is, in addition to being a national minority, also a colony. That is, there are geographical territories within the nation that are de facto controlled and sometimes even occupied militarily by the larger nation, which acts as colonizer of these internal colonies. All national minorities have some of the characteristics of a colony and can be called quasi-colonies but some approximate colonial status more fully. Three examples come to mind: Northern Ireland, where the minority Irish population has been politically and economically dominated by a Protestant ruling class, including virtual military occupation. Puerto Rico, a former classical colony that continues to be an economic "neocolony" of dependent development subject to the U.S. mainland; and Quebec, where most of the population is culturally different from the rest of Canada and is still today subject to the political and economic domination of Ottawa, Toronto, and Wall Street in many ways.

Puerto Rico is a source of cheap labor for North American investors there. It also exports its unemployed to the mainland where Puerto Ricans typically find themselves in the lower strata of the labor force, and as a "reserve army" of under- and unemployed low-

skilled workers. Puerto Rican demands for statehood and independence reflect long-standing movements of struggle against colonial
conditions. Quebec is instructive in another way. This "colony" has
improved its economic condition to such a degree in recent years
that nationalist calls for independence, which are decreasingly successful, are less a reflection of Third World suffering than of a drive
for political autonomy by its own "native bourgeoisie."

A host of other countries exist in which north-south differences
are such that the south, or at least parts of it (as in Italy and the
former Yugoslavia), suffer such economic disadvantages that they are
often described (by local leaders at least) as colonies. Conversely,
insofar as the north sees them as a drag on economic development,
there are movements (as in northern Italy) to sever the advanced part
from its "backward" portions. When disadvantages coincide with historical ethnic differences, as in the former Austro-Hungarian empire
and its successor states, national independence movements invariably result, and indeed carry on generation after generation. Given a
lack of a transcending, overall national identity or a government
prepared to impose one (as in Stalin's, or more moderately in Tito's
day), centrifugal forces may, and do, plunge nations into civil wars.
The list of such wars since the collapse of central authority in the
former Soviet Union and the former Yugoslavia speaks volumes
about the consequences of the political and economic suppression
or colonization of national minorities.

Many countries today contain large numbers of immigrant
ethnic minorities, frequently several of them. Immigration takes
many forms. Slavery and indentured servitude or peonage, while
common throughout history, is now outlawed, even though still
practiced in a few countries. Poverty-stricken Third World people
are "pushed" to seek work in the industrially advanced countries,
which seek such workers to augment their own labor forces in sectors of the economy ranging from farm labor to garment manufac-
ture to information technology. During boom periods skilled
workers and carefully selected unskilled workers (for example,

domestics) are encouraged. During periods of economic woe, "underpaid migrant workers...become an important resource for employers" in order to cut costs and undermine domestic labor standards.[4] When Third World countries suffer high levels of unemployment (in part due to the destruction of village agriculture), "exporting unemployment by force and/or actively stimulating emigration has been a major policy."[5] Moreover, these emigrants, even though poorly paid in the receiving country, send funds home, thereby helping to keep the sending country's economy afloat. There are some 5 million Mexicans working in the United States without documents, the Mexican government estimated in 1996. They send home $3.6 billion, Mexico's third largest source of foreign exchange after petroleum and sweatshop factories. Most "nations of immigrants" have been founded largely on the surplus labor of other (mainly European) countries. Only recently have some traditionally labor-exporting countries such as Italy and Japan reversed their course to become net importers of labor.

In many countries some members of particular "outgroups" characteristically become small merchants, or "intermediate minorities." Formerly Jews, and today Asians in a number of countries are examples. Typically, merchant ethnicities concentrate at first in marginal businesses considered undesirable by the majority population, for example, pawnbrokers. As such they are perceived as exploiters or parasites by their neighbors, who are often poverty-stricken and seek scapegoats. Later, more educated generations find themselves in the lower levels of the civil service (teachers, social workers) and are seen as agents of the power structure, and are again scapegoated. The "Court Jew," vizier to czars and presidents alike, represents the upper stratum of this category. He (usually a male) in particular and Jews in general then suffer the consequences of mistakes made by their employers. Historically, this scapegoating has been welcomed, and even encouraged, by many elites.

In any society, certain jobs are stigmatized as dirty or undesirable and people must be found to do them. Rather than rewarding people for doing these jobs, what happens is that some people are stigmatized so as to exclude them from other jobs and force them into the "dirty" work. The process then becomes circular: those who are stigmatized do the dirty jobs, and those who do the dirty jobs are stigmatized. Immigrants and racial minorities, especially those with limited educations and skills, are easiest to push into dirty work. Once there, it is hard to break out and up, since the incomes generated by such work are insufficient to acquire the educational tools needed for upward mobility.

The United States is unique in containing within its borders two very large "racial" immigrant minorities, African Americans, and Mexican Americans (by far the largest group of Hispanic background). While nations do differ in the degree to which racial-immigrant minorities suffer disadvantages, almost all racially identifiable immigrant groups suffer more than other immigrants. Even when their economic position improves, their visibility (sometimes also based on cultural differences) keeps them vulnerable to being scapegoated for all sorts of social ills. The larger the number, the more different the culture, and the tighter the labor market, the more hostile will be the reception. The manipulation of such hostility by political forces results in the development of movements with a "nativist" or xenophobic tinge throughout the world.

It is evident that the historical "luxury" of having a homogeneous ethnic population is a thing of the past in the age of "global" or transnational economies. The rate and level of internal conflict between dominant and minority groups appears on the rise almost everywhere. Why has it been so hard to resolve such conflicts? And why has it been so difficult to do more than minimally improve the relative position of most minorities, whether they are aborigines, minority nationalities, ghettoized "internal colony" dwellers, or simply immigrants?

What is often missing from discussions of "ethnic" or "race" relations is that minority status intersects with class issues. Specifically, the subordinate status of minorities, regardless of the particular configuration that has developed historically (aborigine, minority nationality, internal colony, immigrant, etc.) is functional to the class structure, or the way the economy is organized, and the way the state and other institutions function to protect the existing class structure. Bigotry rationalizes discrimination, which is functional to the dominant ethnicity and particularly to the minority of that ethnicity that actually holds the reins of power (political, social, and economic) in its hands. The present economy requires a certain amount of cheap labor. It also requires a stratum of "middlemen" to service the poor. Discrimination creates a population forced to take those kinds of work. A certain level of un- and underemployment is functional as a threat to the employed in order to keep labor costs down. The disproportional negative effects of economic change on minority populations creates such a "reserve army of labor."

The larger social order requires scapegoats to divert the attention of broader layers of dissatisfied people away from the real source of their troubles. When the media constantly connect the "dysfunctional" behaviors of the poor and the unemployed to minority status, that scapegoating is accomplished. And when minorities come to see other minorities as their main enemies, rather than targeting the power structure, scapegoating works to divert attention from the real problem. Scapegoating is truly "the socialism of fools."

What are the different "agendas" that modern states use to "deal" with their ethnic, racial, cultural, linguistic, religious, immigrant, and national (and usually combinations of these) minorities? The agendas range from outright extermination to the attempt to create a multinational, culturally pluralistic society, to total integration. Although total extermination (genocide) has come close, no strategy has fully "worked" in terms of success within its own assumptions.

It has sometimes been said that fascism as a theory and movement is not inherently genocidal, although when its imperialistic ambitions lead it to war against another nation, large-scale killing of those nationals (including civilians) is inevitable. However, the Nazi brand of fascism made the extermination of Jews and other "inferior races" central to its program (see chapter 5). Moreover, should "enemy aliens" live within fascist society, they are pretty much doomed to physical extinction, too, as are political dissidents regardless of their ethnicity. The nationalist rhetoric of fascist societies requires total unity, and demonizes and dehumanizes the "enemy" (not that this is unique to fascism, just that it is significantly more pronounced, partly because there are no forces within the country that might call for a moderation of such extreme rhetoric).

For the Nazis, in contrast to the Italian fascists, racism and specifically anti-Semitism were present from the first. Ur-Nazi writers such as Oswald Spengler had previewed Hitler's more fully developed and more vehement racism and anti-Semitism years before the publication of the Nazi bible, *Mein Kampf.* The genocidal character of the Nazi state is more than amply documented. Suffice it to summarize: The Nazi genocides "likely cost the lives of about 16,300,000 people: nearly 5,300,000 Jews, 260,000 Gypsies, 10,500,000 Slavs, and 220,000 homosexuals as well as another 170,000 handicapped Germans."[6] This is apart from the large-scale murders, directly or by starvation, of political opponents, hostages, forced laborers, prisoners of war, and others not mainly targeted for what were considered "eugenic" reasons.

The National Security or authoritarian state in the Third World presents a more complex picture, although tolerance of minorities and minority nationalities is rare. Some states, like Korea, are fairly homogeneous, so aside from some religious minorities, it is a nonissue. At the other extreme are countries with large minorities where genocidal strategies, formal or informal, have been and still are being used.

In 1971, the Pakistan government under Agha Mohammed Khan attacked East Pakistan (now Bangladesh) with the objective of driving the Hindu population into India, and subordinating East Pakistan to West Pakistan permanently, a policy nowadays termed "ethnic cleansing." "Within 267 days," writes the "democide" scholar R. J. Rummel, the Pakistan state was responsible for killing "about

1,500,000 people, turned another 10 million into refugees who fled to India, provoked a war with India, incited a counter-genocide of 150,000 non-Bengalis, and lost East Pakistan."[7] This was just prior to the events briefly described in chapter 2.

Better known in the West was what has been termed the first real genocide of this century, the carefully planned virtual extermination of the Armenians by Turkey, which was launched in 1915. Estimates vary, but the figure of between 300,000 and 1,400,000 in one year alone will have to suffice to give some idea of the magnitude of this catastrophe. Altogether, nearly 2 million Armenians were killed between 1915 and 1923 including most of the 200,000 or so Armenians who had been drafted into the Turkish army. The nationalist spirit of the "Young Turks," who were bent on creating a unified modern nation uncluttered by minorities, was part of the equation. The other part was the very economic, cultural, and intellectual success of the hardworking, classically "middleman-minority" Armenians, a frightening parallel to the history of the German Jews. By 1922 only about 5 percent of the 1914 Armenian population was left alive in Turkey.

Turkey was then neither a fascist state nor a "national security state." In 1913 a group of nationalist "Young Turks" had conducted a coup d'etat and aligned the country with Germany for the forthcoming war. The extermination of the Armenians, done in the name of national unity, followed. Following their defeat in the war, the Young Turk regime collapsed, a sultan was restored, and portions of Turkey were occupied by the Allies. In May 1919 a rebel nationalist government was set up by the future dictator, Mustafa Kemal (later called Ataturk). His regime continued the attacks on the Armenians. In 1922 the Turks and the Greeks agreed to a population swap. Massacres were conducted by each against the other, continuing the legacy of hatred between Greeks and Turks that remains even today. The secular Kemalist state engaged in a series of "modernizing" measures by fiat including the elimination of the Arab alphabet, Muslim schools, the Islamic legal system, and the wearing of the veil. From a historical point of view, it probably makes more sense to compare the secular-military dictatorship of Turkey to the Bonapartist style of the South Korean military, or to Egypt's Col. Gamal Abdel Nasser, who overthrew King Faruk in 1952 and engineered the removal of British troops a few years later. Nevertheless, Turkey continues to be plagued by internal unrest mainly in Kurdish regions. The Turkish "agenda" with regard to minorities appears to have changed from that of 1915 only in that outright extermination is no longer feasible. However, the Turkish state has engaged in extensive "ethnic cleansing" of Kurdish areas, including the destruction of thousands of villages. Since 1992 between 2.5 and 5 million Kurds have been forcibly expelled from their homelands and scattered into cities as part of a long-term strategy of what amounts to "ethnocide": the deliberate attempt to destroy an entire culture without necessarily exterminating all of its people.

In many "Third World" countries today the issue is not nation building, with the sometimes associated "need" to eliminate minority nationalities. Instead, it is the need to sustain minorities (mainly the aborigine population, or indigenes) as a source of cheap labor to work on plantations, in mines, and otherwise to supply marginal labor. But "marginal" is only the appearance, since "the immiserated are...central to the capitalist productive process"[8] because their participation at the lower levels of the global economy is essential, not only as household servants for the local bourgeoisie, but more importantly as workers in the Maquiladora sweatshop factory system. Their forced expulsion from village lands by the state and agribusiness leaves few avenues for survival: moving to the urban centers and eking out an existence in low-level factory work, or, in the case of many women, prostitution; or migrating to "El Norte" or other "First World" countries. These migrants, whether domestic or international, are disproportionally members of indigenous populations. In Latin America they often continue to speak indigenous languages and do not speak Spanish.

The colonial period was characterized by the large-scale

destruction of native populations by gunfire, disease, starvation, and the ravages of forced labor. Even after independence the story in country after country south of the Rio Grande has been the continuing enslavement, really or virtually, of native populations in the service of local military strongmen, local elite bourgeoisies, and later, of foreign investors. In many countries where bourgeois revolutions secured independence from Spain, suffrage was so restricted that "Indians" were effectively barred from the political process.

Many millions of indigenous people who escape the fate of living in urban slums survive only marginally in jungle or hill areas, always subject to the whim of the local military. The explosion of the Zapatista Army of National Liberation in Chiapas State, Mexico, in 1994 was only the most graphic symptom of the continuing suffering, and resistance, of poor peasants throughout all of Central and South America, who are disproportionally of aborigine background. The Zapatistas of today are concentrated in Mayan regions and speak at least four different native languages. In Guatemala, too, "Indians" have borne the brunt of fighting against the dictatorship that overthrew the elected government of Jacobo Arbenz in 1954, and have suffered the consequences. The government has used napalm and phosphorous bombs, massacred unarmed civilians, utilized death squads, "disappeared" real or suspected oppositionists, etc.

The legacy of the Inquisition also contributed to the widespread animosity held by those of European Catholic descent not only for the indigenes, but even for some of European background. Although there are fewer than a half-million Jews south of the U.S. border, anti-Semitism is widespread. "The stereotype of Jews as subversives persists today, even in secular countries such as Argentina. The generals who led Argentina's dirty war (1976–1983) attacked Jews as quintessential subversives."[9]

In sum, whether the purpose is nation building (sometimes linked to one or another religion) or the exploitation of labor, authoritarian states show little if any tolerance for ethnic minorities, especially those who are "racially" or religiously different.

This agenda is linked, though not always rooted, in the nature of revolutions against corrupt feudal regimes by military elements, "from the top," as in Turkey. The military acts as a "surrogate" for the bourgeoisie in the process of development. In this sense the army functions as a Bonapartist force, as a bridge to a more modern society. "In societies where everyone is tardy, the military is prompt. Where the population is ragged, the soldiers are neatly uniformed. Where indecisiveness reigns supreme, the military can take direct action."[10] But the price for social cohesion is the suppression or elimination of elements that don't fit in, sectors of the population that are deemed unreliable because they are culturally or otherwise different. The more power a state has—and a military state has a great deal—the more likely it is to massacre in cold blood those it controls.

Of all dictatorships, the Stalinist state was unique in that a supposedly positive policy toward minorities was encoded in Soviet law, and was, at least in theory, based on the actual writings of Lenin, Stalin, and (according to them) Marxism.

In 1914 Lenin wrote an essay "The Right of Nations to Self-Determination," in which he attacked the position of others within the broader European socialist movement, most particularly the Polish and German Marxist Rosa Luxemburg, on the subject of minority nationalities. Lenin saw the national state as the form of political structure under which capitalism can best develop. He advocated both the independence of nations that find themselves subordinated to larger national bodies, as under tsarism, and nationalities subject to colonial masters, because he saw the historical struggle against feudal restrictions and colonialism as a progressive struggle, and the bourgeosie as a progressive formation vis-à-vis feudalism (as had Marx and Engels). The bourgeoisie organizes nationalist movements that have as their goals the formation of independent bourgeois states. Such movements should be supported by the working class and its proletarian party, a position that Luxemburg, a consistent internationalist, felt was flawed. The controversy between Lenin, Luxemburg, and a third approach, that of the Austro-Marxists led by Otto Bauer, while intrinsically interesting, is secondary to the present discussion.[11]

Stalin's famous essay "Marxism and the National Question" actually preceded Lenin's major piece by one year, but it was significantly based on Lenin's earlier pronouncements on the nationalities issue. In this essay, Stalin argued that "no one (has) the right to *forcibly* interfere in the life of the nation, to *destroy* its schools and other institutions, to *violate* its habits and customs, to *repress* its language, or *curtail* its rights,"[12] a sentiment totally contradicted by his later actions. Nations within a larger nation had the right to federation status, or to regional autonomy (both later incorporated into the Soviet Union's structure), but also the right to secede.

The slogan of self-determination for subject nations worked all too well as the civil war that accompanied the establishment of the Soviet state developed. Finland proclaimed independence in April 1917, even before the revolution. By the end of 1918, Forman tells us, thirteen new states had been created in a centrifugal process not unlike that of the early 1990s following the collapse of the Soviet regime. "[C]laims for a right to self-determination came into conflict with the revolution itself.... Most ... of the regimes ruling the new states were anti-socialist," so they became bases for Western intervention.[13] In 1920 Stalin repudiated the principle of secession. He began rapidly to subordinate the structures and cultures of the Soviet Union's "autonomous" republics to the need to create a cohesive, overarching "socialist" state, one that was now suffering isolation in the absence of revolution in the West. Soon, the Third, or Communist International would begin to mold its member parties throughout the world to fit the foreign policy needs of the Soviet Union, as interpreted by Stalin and his bureaucracy. And that included, quite importantly, these parties' positions on the minorities in their own countries. As good an example as any other are the twists and turns of the Communist Party USA with regard to the "Negro Question."[14]

By the early 1930s, Stalin and his colleagues had reversed the old socialist dictum that the national question had to be seen in socialist terms. Instead, "socialism" as practiced in the Soviet Union had become synonymous with national unity. This permitted Stalin to deal with national minorities depending on their degree of loyalty. The consequence was that over the years tens to hundreds of thousands of people of specific nationalities (Cossacks, Ukrainians, Estonians, Volga Germans, and others) were murdered or intentionally starved to death, or sent into an internal exile under the most dire conditions. Interspersed thoughout the period since 1917 has been an on-again, off-again policy of outright anti-Semitism, even though an autonomous republic, Birobidjan, was set up for Jews (albeit in Siberia) in which the Yiddish language survived.

In sum, Stalinist policy toward minorities failed to "solve" the "nationalities question." Due to its repressive and manipulative character, it succeeded in driving the quest for genuine self-determination and equality by minorities underground. When the Stalin bureaucracy then collapsed, a storm of secessionist movements was unleashed. Many of these movements soon became ultranationalistic and quasi-fascist, resulting in the persecution of minorities within the new secessionist states themselves, and still more conflict. Stalin's legacy therefore continues to haunt the peoples of the former Soviet Union long after his death.

We turn now to the "liberal democracies" of the West. Extermination is not an acceptable policy for modern bourgeois states, although they may look the other way, or even encourage it, in other states. Minority nationalities organized in some federal or autonomous form are rare. Secession, though frequently discussed and sometimes fought for, as in the case of the Basques, has really not been permitted in any modern state.

The range of policy options and debates, however, is quite extensive. There are states (Germany, and, paradoxically, Israel) that base citizenship on membership in the ethnicity, the "Volk," on the "law of blood," so that there is a legal "right of return" for those who belong, even though they may not have lived in that respective country for a century, and may not even speak the language. There are other countries, such as France, which are committed to a form of secularism in which to be a citizen means to be totally integrated. This implies censure, and even persecution, of ethnicities (e.g., Moslems) who do not "look" to fit in (head coverings for women, long dresses, strange foods, other customs unlike those of the nation as a whole). In Germany, nationalism insofar as it exists (and of course it still does in many parts of the population, despite the grim history of this century) is based on ethnicity. In France, nationalism, usually considered simply patriotism there, is of a civil or secular style, connected to the tradition of the French Revolution. Still other countries (the United States, Canada) that are nations of immigrants straddle the ethnicity fence between integration and cultural pluralism, with debates about the meaning of these concepts a constant. Such debates are also increasing in other countries as the number of immigrants increases. U.S. and Canadian agendas are complicated by the presence of "Native American" or "First" nations that are true national minorities, and also by the presence of large populations of racial minorities (and in Canada, one entire province differing markedly from the rest of the nation in language, religion, and history).

What are minorities to do? In most modern societies, minority movements are strategically split between "nationalists" who advocate political autonomy in some form, versus "integrationists" who believe that given enough pressure, their group will attain equality and become fully part of the parent nation. The Jewish "community" in pre-Hitler Germany, for example, was split into a majority that defined itself as "Germans of the Jewish faith" and often went out of its way to prove its loyalty to the kaiser, versus a minority that was Zionist in inspiration, that is, saw itself to one degree or another as strangers, exiles in Germany.

Within each of these broad strategies there are many subtypes, some more radical and socialistic, others more culturally oriented, some advocating the tactics of direct action, others the more moderate road of participation in the normal political process. Zionism, as a nationalist movement, has always been split between a more labor or socialistic orientation, versus a narrower, more culturalist or religious tendency. Similarly, the black movement in the United States has long been divided between integrationists (including socialists such as A. Philip Randolph) and nationalists, who have ranged in type from the "back to Africa" movement of Marcus Garvey to the contemporary Nation of Islam. The integrationists have ranged in their strategies from the lobbying and court fights of the NAACP to the nonviolent direct action of Martin Luther King Jr. while the nationalists have advocated everything from self-help to demanding a geographical territory for African Americans within the United States. In the late 1920s the Communist Party advocated the creation of a Black Soviet Republic in the "Black Belt" of the South, in line with Stalin's thinking at the time.

As for the state, it must balance the fact that minorities are functional for capital (in terms of their roles in the labor market and as scapegoats) against the disruptions that inevitably result from being oppressed. The more people in the streets, the more reforms, according to Piven and Cloward's excellent study,[15] but only up to a point. When protest begins to endanger the stability of the society in a serious way, by which is meant the survival of the power structure and the state, severe repression short of fascism (but perhaps falling into the category of "friendly fascism"—see chapter 3) can result. Once the Black Panther Party came to be seen as a serious threat by the state, it was effectively destroyed through infiltration by agents provocateurs, endless court cases, and outright murder.

Although modern states vary in their assumptions about the nature of citizenship, particularly now that they face increasing immigration and large numbers of refugees, there is a set of common assumptions that dominate the minorities discourse in the West. Racist theories about the inherent inferiority of certain groups do persist, and make periodic comebacks (even in the guise of science) and pose political dangers, as currently in France and Austria, but these ideas have been generally discredited and are no longer dominant. A more common view is that the presence of large numbers of immigrants, ethnic minorities, and indeed the entire project called cultural pluralism (or multiculturalism) endangers national cohesiveness, leads to conflict, and more generally threatens to undermine "civilization." Blatantly racist movements as well as this more "respectable" approach are often, if not always, responses to rapid social change, insecure times, and bad economic conditions, all contexts that makes scapegoating popular.

By contrast to such a "fear of the other" is the model that Omi and Winant call the "ethnicity paradigm." This is the most common view in social scientific circles. This model proceeds on two assumptions: first, that all minority groups are ethnic in nature and face basically similar problems, and second, that given appropriate social policies (particularly opening educational and occupational opportunities) all groups will eventually replicate the history of previous groups and become fitted for citizenship, or at minimum achieve equal social standing. Even if they cannot be citizens, they can be like us in every other way. It follows that if a group continues to be disadvantaged, it is either because opportunities are still blocked, the case for legislation, or that there is something wrong with their method of adjustment, the case for blaming their maladaptive culture. The former approach is that of classical reform liberalism; the latter approach is useful for scapegoating and fits into right-wing populist demagogy. What is wrong with this theory, as Omi and Winant make clear, is that different groups have quite different histories, bring different kinds of capital with them (money and human talent), and differ in their numbers and in their access to the opportunity structure (the labor market) when they arrive (whether from abroad or from some other part of the country, for instance, the southern United States). And, to reiterate, minorities identifiable as racially different have a tougher time given the legacy of racism that exists in virtually all "democracies." In short, the playing field is not level.

Minorities constitute a challenge to the kind of national identity that is fostered by the modern state, which requires some semblance of cohesiveness in order to do business. Modern nations were formed in the context of the development of modern capitalism, as Lenin observed. They are based on rationality, science, secularism, in short, the Enlightenment. The inherent tendency of the Enlightenment is to undermine ethnic fragmentation, to amalgamate all people within a nation into a common project, one that is linked to commerce and, presumably, prosperity. The French version of the ethnicity paradigm, that of assimilation, is the logical one for modern society. As minorities prosper, they lose their ethnic characteristics except for a few culinary items: the bagel has now joined the hamburger and the pizza as an American staple. And this, according to the theory, is as it should be, and the state should be promoting this road to the future.

But it is not working out that way. "The world is now in a period of desecularization. Wherever one turns, whether to the industrialized world or to the less-developed nations, the religious quest is newly invigorated. Gone is the sense that time is on the side of the secular; instead fundamentalists strut with ever-greater confidence across the world stage, believing that time and tide are on their side."[16] How can this be? How is it that virtually all modern secular states are facing this kind of cultural backlash to one degree or another?

The bourgeois state is a class state, and as such it cannot "solve" the minorities or nationalities "question," because it cannot solve the class question. At the root of the rejection of modernism, of the Enlightenment by those who distrust secularism is a deep, if subconscious, malaise about living in an oppressive, atomizing, class society. In the absence of large-scale progressive movements that once created a sense of community for many, ethnic identity (including religion) fills the spiritual vacuum by providing a sense of community. Ethnic (or racial) pride provides an island of safety in an anomic world. Much of this is harmless, although it also could be said that it is an evasion of responsibility for social change, that it is an "opiate of the people," to borrow Marx's phrase. The problem is that too often one person's ethnic pride and community loyalty may result in another person's ethnic destruction. The blatant anti-Semitism that occasionally crops up in extremist black nationalist circles, which exactly mirrors the anti-Semitism of white supremacist antiblack hate groups is a tragic commentary on how easily the need for ethnic pride can lead to bitter conflicts between groups (in this case blacks and Jews) that logically should be allied in a common struggle for equal rights. So the wars between ethnicities, religions, and races go on, and continue to testify to the failure of modern capitalist society to create that liberty, equality, and fraternity, that it was supposed to be about, though of course it never was about that. It was always about making money, which has become, like Communism, a god that has failed for a great many people.

In this context, the modern state is stuck in the middle. It cannot provide the level of reforms that would lead to full equality because it must protect the interests of the dominant class. Yet it cannot brutally suppress the movements for minority rights either, for that would generate too much disaffection. As always, the state is caught between using the carrot and the stick.

## NOTES

1. Michael Omi and Howard Winant, *Racial Formation in the United States* (New York: Routledge, 1994).

2. Stephen Steinberg, *The Ethnic Myth* (Boston: Beacon Press, 1989), 53.

3. Omi and Winant, *Racial Formation in the United States*, 44–47. See also Robert Blauner, *Racial Oppression in America* (New York: Harper and Row, 1972).

4. James D. Cockcroft, *Outlaws In the Promised Land* (New York: Grove Press, 1986), 115.

5. Goeran Therborn, *Why Some Peoples Are More Unemployed Than Others* (London: Verso, 1986), 82. See also David L. Wilson, "Do Maquiladoras Matter?" *Monthly Review* (October 1997).

6. R. J. Rummel, *Death By Government* (New Brunswick, N.J.: Transaction Publishers, 1994), 119.

7. Ibid., 315–16.

8. James D. Cockcroft, *Mexico* (New York: Monthly Review Press, 1983), 233.

9. Judith Laikin Elken, "Colonial Legacy of Anti-Semitism," *Report on the Americas* 25, no. 4 (February 1992): 5.

10. Irving Louis Horowitz, *Three Worlds of Development* (New York: Oxford University Press, 1966), 267.

11. For discussions of this issue see, among others, Stephen Eric Bronner, *Rosa Luxemburg* (University Park, Pa.: Pennsylvania State University Press, 1997), chap. 2; Norbert Leser, "The Austro-Marxists and the Nationalities Question," in *Vienna: The World of Yesterday*, ed. Bronner and F. Peter Wagner (Amherst, N.Y.: Humanity Books, 1997); and, particularly, Michael Forman, *Nationalism and the International Labor Movement* (University Park, Pa.: Pennsylvania State University Press, 1998).

12. Quoted in Forman, ibid., 129.

13. Ibid., 132.

14. See, for example, William A. Nolan, *Communism Versus the Negro* (Chicago: Henry Regnery, 1951); Irving Howe and Lewis Coser, *The American Communist Party: A Critical History* (New York: Praeger, 1962). For the Party's views see, for example, James S. Allen, *The Negro Question in the United States* (New York: International Publishers, 1936); William Z. Foster, "On the Question of Negro Self-Determination," *Political Affairs* (January 1947); James S. Allen, *History of the Communist Party of the United States* (New York: International Publishers, 1952); Benjamin Davis, *The Negro People on the March* (New York: New Century Publishers, 1956).

15. Frances Fox Piven and Richard A. Cloward, *Poor People's Movements* (New York: Vintage Books, 1979).

16. Leonard Fein, "Israel's Un-Orthodox Battle," *Nation*, July 7, 1997.

# EPILOGUE

# THE NEW LEVIATHAN?

*His bared teeth strike terror. Firebrands stream from his mouth. Out of his nostrils comes smoke. His breath ignites coals. Power leaps before him. He is as though cast hard; he does not totter. His heart is cast hard as stone. No sword that overtakes him can prevail, nor spear, nor missile, nor lance. There is no one on land who can dominate him. He is king over all proud beasts.*

—from Job 40[1]

If the autonomy of the state is relative, then it will vary depending on the relationship between and within classes in a given period. Is the modern state becoming relatively more or less autonomous? In *Global Capitalism: The New Leviathan*, Ross and Trachte examine the changes in the relationships among capital, labor, and the state in recent years. These changes, as old-fashioned "monopoly capitalism" moves toward "global capitalism," they conclude, "shifts the balance of class forces toward capital, and one of the results is decline in the relative autonomy of the state."[2] The state, the authors maintain, was relatively more autonomous under monopoly capitalism than in the present era because there were important differences among the fractions of capital, which the state needed to mediate or reconcile in the overall interest of the system. But today's global firms are far more powerful in their impact on all fractions of capital, and therefore have far more leverage over state policy. This is for the simple reason that they are almost infinitely capable of moving, of withdrawing investment from areas that are sympathetic to labor (or for that matter are sloppy in their banking methods, or are so corrupt that it interferes with investment, or for any other reason). They can force rollbacks in social welfare, extort belt-tightening via their international banking system (which controls loans), and they can even force the resignations of governments by the threat of fiscal punishment. They do this via such mechanisms as the World Bank, the International Monetary Fund, and other such agencies, which they control for all practical purposes.

The resources available to consumer, neighborhood, and labor groups for fighting against their deteriorating living standards, working conditions, and even the destruction of the environment seem far outweighed by the power that is in the hands of the global managers of investment. The fear of capital flight, combined with the domination of state apparatuses (governments) by conservatives (or even social democrats who have made their peace with capital or have no choice but to accommodate to capital) has weakened organized labor. Furthermore, these same global capitalists also dominate the ideological or cultural apparatuses that continue to "sell" the idea that the "free market" is the only option for a decent way of life. The collapse of Communism appears to many to have left no alternative.

This is a grim, Leviathan-like picture, one in which even the notion of a friendly fascism seems outmoded. Of course business interests, and the states with which they are intermingled, view this picture of their global hegemony positively. Their argument is that globalization must inevitably lead to prosperity, even though some countries, parts of countries, or strata of the population (namely, the lower-income and working-class and peasant groups) will have to suffer a bit for a while as the Calvinistic price of postponing gratification in order to reap the rewards of hard work in the future. The evidence for this optimistic prognosis is not encouraging, however.

It is true that in a number of "Third World" countries there has been significant growth in the middle class of entrepreneurs, professionals, and state sector employees. But the public sector has never been small in such countries, since a large state infrastructure has been necessary for a long time to service the needs of capital, whether local or international (supplying the infrastructure to train workers, provide a stable financial system, police the labor force, and build certain essential technical capabilities such as reliable transportation and communications systems). Much of the growth in the private sector has been for the purpose of meeting multinational corporate needs. Investment oriented to the growth of really independent national capitalist classes (the import substitution model) has in most cases been abandoned in favor of export-driven industrialization. Although much growth continues to be of a "dependent" kind, there has also been an increase in the development of a handful of nationally based conglomerates (headed by billionaires), as local capitalists, aligned with their authoritarian or semiauthoritarian states, take advantage of the general redistribution of wealth upward. In countries like Chile, Mexico, Peru, Thailand, and even quasi-"communist" countries like China great fortunes have been made in both industrial and financial enterprises, at the expense of the large majority of the population. However, as we saw in 1997, there can be overexpansion (with corresponding overcapacity). Indebtedness to the international banking community can increase and lead to abrupt crises in financial markets, sudden disinvestment (an outflow of capital sometimes literally overnight), and consequent growth in unemployment even beyond the usual high rates.

One of the consequences of the increasing strength of the international financial "community" of banking and industrial capital relative to states that at one point were vulnerable to pressures from unions and other movements is the drive toward the privatization of public facilities ranging from state-owned telephone, gas, and electric, and even automobile industries, to healthcare and governmental retirement systems. This is true in both "advanced" and "developing" nations, although these moves do not go unchallenged. In Puerto Rico there were large-scale protests in 1997 against attempts by the government to sell the publicly owned telephone company, the twelfth-largest in the United States. Allegedly in the interest of greater efficiency, these privatizations inevitably worsen the living standards of most people as the cost of services shifts from a society-wide base to the individual consumer, who must also pay for the profit without which privatization would make no sense. They also function to curtail the "capacity to deal with problems, such as environmental destruction, that requires social planning over many future decades....Privatization shifts power from bodies that can take social costs...into account to those that cannot because of their dedication to profits."[3]

U.S. advocates of "globalization" laud such policies as the North American Free Trade Agreement (NAFTA) as heralding a new prosperity on both sides of the border. However, as imports from Third World countries increase, the pressure on U.S. workers also grows. Employers facing union-organizing drives threaten to close their plants and move. The number of "sweatshops" (poor safety conditions, violations of wages and hours legislation, etc.) increases in order to compete with low-priced imports based on low-wage foreign labor. Environmental degradation in Third World countries increases. Wages there also fall as companies threaten to move to still lower-wage areas. Human rights, including the right of labor to organize, are sidetracked in the interest of profitable trade deals. Inequality within and between countries grows.

The picture in the United States is symptomatic, although by no means the extreme. The top 1 percent of U.S. households now owns more wealth than the bottom 90 percent, while more than one-quarter of U.S. workers are in jobs that pay wages below the official poverty line. Large corporations downsize in the interest of maximizing the short-term bottom line, and more people are forced into low-paid independent contracting, and into other kinds of contingent (temp, part-time, etc.) labor. While it is true that more Americans than ever "own" their own homes and participate in the stock market, more Americans than ever are also declaring personal bankruptcy. Financial institutions actually control the mutual and pension funds in which individuals minimally participate, and home "ownership" really means paying half or more of net income to lending institutions in borrowing costs. More and more people are one paycheck away from financial disaster. As one observer summarizes it, even though conditions have improved for many in the upper and upper-middle strata, "life has become more precarious, and insecurity greater, for vast segments of the working population."[4] In this context the state, rather than moving independently, toward more autonomy, in order to resolve some of the conflicts that this development inevitably generates, has been the handmaiden of this strategy. A bipartisan, right-centrist consensus has encouraged the dismantling of the New Deal, the deregulation of business, the privatization of health care, and cutbacks in a host of measures that were originally designed to accommodate protest movements ranging from labor to civil rights to environmentalism.

Are Ross and Trachte then right in their description of the declining autonomy of the state? In the "emerging market" Third World states, which are highly dependent on world financial institutions and markets, this is undoubtedly true, as was pointed out in chapter 2. Yet a number of observers have argued that this does not always follow in the "advanced" part of the world. Indeed, without a strong state presence the implementation of a global marketplace would not be possible. Just as colonial expansion in the interest of trade could not have taken place without the protection, if not the outright sponsorship, of European states, today's state "has been a key agent in the implementation of global processes."[5] Moreover, as Wood argues, behind "every transnational corporation is a national base, which depends on its local state to sustain its viability and on other states to give it access to other markets and other labor forces."[6]

Consequently the state continues to be essential to the functioning of the multinational capitalist economic system.

But this does not mean that the state is autonomous. As national capitals become more dependent on worldwide economic conditions (not just general conditions but also specifically such fiscal aspects of the economy as interest rates) the state may appear to become more autonomous because it must act on behalf of all of a nation's capitalist class fractions. It must therefore be able to enact policies that regulate or even constrain capital (for example by forcing an increase in interest rates, or by allowing some financial institutions to go bankrupt, or by devaluating the currency) in the interest of its overall survival. But this apparently increasing autonomy develops within the parameters of the requirements of capital in an overall sense.

Take environmental degradation. Few governments foster serious regulation of the environment when that challenges the economic interests of a particular national capitalist interest in the context of global competition. "Trends such as the globalization of capital and growing competition among nations...bring in their wake both burgeoning environmental problems and increases in disaster severity" (as in the 1984 Bhopal [India] chemical spill disaster).[7]

Does globalization mark a departure, a new phenomenon in the history of capitalism? Clearly not. Marx and Engels, in the 1848 *Manifesto*, described the phenomenon clearly: "The need of a constantly expanding market for its products chases the bourgeoisie over the whole surface of the globe. It must nestle everywhere, settle everywhere, establish connections everywhere." In that era, when both people and goods moved freely across national borders, without passports or customs duty, foreign capital as a percent of GNP often exceeded its rates today. Henwood argues that economic internationalization is actually less in degree than it was a century ago. Three-quarters of U.S. investments abroad are concentrated in richer, industrialized countries such as Canada. Multinational corporations account for only about 15 percent of the world's industrial output.

At the same time the financial structure of "globalization" has changed in several ways. Currency trading is expanding rapidly. More investment is based on borrowed money. Investors are putting more money into "emerging markets," the new term for the Third World, and technological innovations have lowered the cost of doing business abroad. These factors combined make sudden, dramatic financial crises such as that in 1997 more rather than less likely.

The drive for profit lies at the heart of "globalization" today, as it always has. Investment abroad, as well as the pressure to lower wages and weaken working conditions at home, Henwood proposes, are driven mainly by "demands from Wall Street for fatter profits and higher stock prices."[8] These are reflected in the craze for deregulation, and other policies promoted by politicians to depress wages (such as "ending welfare as we know it" by forcing welfare recipients to take low-wage jobs, thus depressing wages generally among less-skilled workers).

Many corporations face a choice between improving productivity (and profits) by installing expensive capital equipment at home, versus shipping components to low-wage labor abroad for assembly and importing back home. Sixty percent of U.S. merchandise exports to Mexico are to U.S. corporations' branch plants or subcontractors, where goods are finished for shipment elsewhere. The loss of jobs at home is also related to technological change, which means that output per worker increases dramatically. Business, aided by the state, eagerly fosters technological innovation and improved productivity with little regard for environmental impact or the long-term effect on unemployment. It is simply assumed that employment depends on ever increasing output, the sale of which generates both profit and wages. Yet it is logically impossible for every country constantly to increase productivity and sell its products in competition with every other one. Eventually the drive to achieve a competitive edge must also drive wages down, the introduction of improved technology must eventually displace workers, and both factors must at some point limit what people can purchase.

Meanwhile, this constantly increasing production (and consumption) must ultimately deplete natural resources and despoil the environment far beyond the present already depressing picture.

As long as the state is of the parliamentary type, or is in some other way vulnerable to mass pressure, the functioning of the state on behalf of capital can theoretically be altered in such a way as to improve, rather than undermine, living conditions and decrease, rather than increase, the unequal distribution of resources. In short, the state can theoretically be forced to appear to be more autonomous, to act in a more autonomous way that reflects a shift in the balance of class forces away from capital, in a reversal of Ross and Trachte's description of current trends. Movements from below do have an impact, as we saw in 1997 as mass demonstrations put a reduction of the work week (in order to save jobs) on the political agenda not only in France, but throughout the European Union. The state could regulate capital and prevent capital flight if it wanted to (that is, if it were forced), especially in an economically powerful country like the United States. Protection of wages, working conditions, and the environment can be enacted, or maintained. These are political choices. If they are not made it is due to the weakness of the social movements that in the past have promoted them.

The predicament presently facing "movements from below" as they grapple with how to relate to their respective states is rooted in recent history. Following World War II, Western Europe and the United States experienced a period of rapid economic expansion, and capitalist states, especially given the strength of social democratic parties in Europe at least in that period, were forced to make concessions in the interest of labor peace. (In the United States this was less of a problem for the state because the cold war provided an ideological cover for the repression of the Left, especially labor unions tagged with the Communist label.) They could and did pass their profits down the line in the form of many welfare-state benefits, and even in the United States improving living standards for most workers. Unemployment virtually disappeared as well. Piecemeal reform, long advocated by the more moderate wings of social democracy, became the predominant strategy in Europe, and talk of class struggle and transformation to a new socialist society waned. But the improvement of conditions was based on increasing profit and power for capital, especially as multinational financial firms began to be more influential. Social democratic movements, and the unions associated with them, had already bought into the bargain (and had in their complacency failed to recruit new members, especially among women and immigrant groups) and by the late 1970s found themselves with reduced resources in members and above all in militant class consciousness just as capital started to put on the squeeze for more profits. As conditions began to worsen, the leaders of social democratic parties, in their quest for votes, began to move further to the right, toward the middle class and the somewhat more conservative white-collar voters. Their claim to governmental power was that they could run the capitalist state more efficiently, less corruptly, and somewhat more kindly than their conservative rivals, a claim that for all intents and purposes was true. Nevertheless, voters in many countries were persuaded that the costs of social benefits had become too high (in the form of taxes) and that international competition also required cutbacks so as to make investment more attractive. They increasingly voted the social democrats out.

The response was that European social democratic parties moved further to the right, to recapture these voters, in the same way that the U.S. Democratic Party has moved ever more rightward in recent years. This strategy has proved successful in reversing the political tide. But in the process, social democracy found that centrist politics soon turned programmatically into a deeper accommodation to the agenda of business elements. In Britain, the "New" Labour Party under Tony Blair has committed itself to the same stingy fiscal policies as its Conservative predecessors, and on the cultural front is also talking about "family values." None of the Conservatives' previous antiunion legislation will be repealed. The British Labour Party (BLP) has finally admitted what has been in the works for years: that it is a probusiness party. The Italian Communist Party, which renamed itself the Democratic Party of the Left, has stated that "in the present historical circumstances there are no alternatives to the market economy," and has supported some privatization. The German Social Democratic Party, at its executive meeting in September 1997, promised its support for decreasing pension, sickness, and unemployment payments so as to lower employers' costs; to make up the difference, it advocated raising sales taxes, which are disproportionally punitive to lower-income groups. In France, too, where a strong welfare state had extended many benefits, including a national health plan widely regarded as effective and popular, the socialists joined the rush to deregulation and austerity, even in the face of high unemployment rates.

However, there are limits to what will be accepted in the cutbacks imposed by the globalized, deregulated, and reprivatized world. In Italy, Germany, and France, and even in the complacent United States, organized labor has shown signs of an increasing militancy in the past few years. In November and December 1995, there were huge demonstrations and strikes against cutbacks in social services and for more employment in France, despite the fact that the government was being administered by socialists. The consequence was a set of concessions, including a promise to create 700,000 new jobs for younger people. Nevertheless, the socialists went ahead with a plan to privatize France Telecom over the protests of its employees. In Italy, Britain, and France, Labor, or Left coalitions, have been put into office by voters rebelling against conservative cutbacks. But once in power, they face a dilemma. As Singer points out, these parties are faced with a new situation. "What they are being asked now is not to be the reformist managers of capitalist society, not even to manage that society as it is without reforms. They are told to get rid of the conquests achieved by the labor movement...on which their reputation was built and their attraction rested."[9]

It is not much different for the U.S. Democratic Party, whose reputation and attraction was built on the New Deal. The Clinton administration is solidly in the camp of multinational corporate globalization policy. However, there is increasing pressure from organized labor on Democratic legislators, and some of them have resisted and rejected Clintonian proglobalization policies that they and their labor constituents see as damaging to working people. This has resulted in some defeats for President Clinton, and therefore for multinational capital.

The political problem facing "movements from below" takes place in the context of what is widely regarded on the Left as a capitalist crisis. This can be seen in the work of Ross and Trachte, as well as Wood and other Left observers, despite their other disagreements. There are different takes on exactly what causes the crisis. Some point to a diminishment of U.S. economic domination of the capitalist world after Vietnam, and pressure on profits, due to increasing competition. Others emphasize the triumph of pure greed as labor movements decline in influence, in short, increased employer resistance. But there is a more profound question: What crisis? Or, more narrowly, whose crisis? There is a perpetual search for new forms of profit in this age of greater investment mobility across the globe. This has enabled multinational capital to circumvent nation-based regulation and strong labor movements. The profit picture for large businesses has never been better. For them, there is no crisis. The crisis is for the victims, as the labor force is disciplined by the threat of unemployment, and living conditions for masses of people deteriorate. Regardless of the degree of state autonomy, large-scale organization from below with or without social democratic-type parties is the only remedy. In this context, the state becomes the focus of protest strategy insofar as it can be forced to assume a quasi-autonomous role. If it will not do so, it becomes completely identified with capital, and capital itself will have to become the target (in the form of such events as the United Parcel Service strike of 1997, the Bell Atlantic and General Motors strikes of 1998, or public protests against the Nike Corporation's exploitation of Third World women workers, or consumer actions against corporate polluters).

So far, the crisis is that of the victims of globalization, be they factory workers in the rust belt of the Middle West, or small-scale peasant coffee producers in Mexico. So far, capitalism has proven itself overall far more flexible than many Marxists had anticipated and has provided opportunities for upward mobility for tens of millions. Since World War II, capitalism on a world scale has avoided general crisis because it has been able to find new ways to invest, and new markets both at home (given the relative prosperity of the population in the First World, and its consequent ability to expand consumption) and in Third World countries. The collapse of the Second or Communist world, and its willingness to follow the "free market" road, has opened still further markets and avenues for investment. In this context, it is difficult to imagine the collapse of capitalism in the near future, although there will be many low and medium intensity crises such as the "Asian Crisis" of overinvestment, overproduction, and overspeculation that crunched stock markets around the world, or the "Brazilian Crisis" of currency collapse and overnight disinvestment in 1998.

Nevertheless, it is hard to predict what will happen after the near future. The drive for increasing profits at the expense of labor, and the consequent deepening of inequality means that large numbers of people lack the ability to buy and consume at the levels required by constantly expanding production. We then face a classical "overproduction" or "underconsumption" problem, as in the Great Depression of the 1930s. The system will exhaust its ability to expand any further geographically in due course. Given that the logic of capitalism is that it must ever find new sources for investment, and new markets, and as these sources become exhausted and saturated, the probability is that crises will intensify.

How will the parties of the "Left" react? The U.S. Democratic Party, as well as European social democrats, will have to choose between further compromise with capital, in which case voters, especially those from the lower-income strata, are likely to turn against them. But where will they go? The real danger is that in Europe they will move to the ultraright, to the nationalist and xeno-phobic anti-immigration parties such as the National Front in France, which already controls several city governments, and the "Folk Union" party in Germany, which now has seats in one state legislature. In the United States there is the extreme Right in or just outside the Republican Party, where isolationist, supermoralistic "Christian" and thinly disguised racist rhetoric is dominant. It will be necessary for the Left to "mobilize on a mass scale...reinvent a socialist project for our times,"[10] in order to outflank such reactionary movements, something that is very probably outside the will and the capacity of the present parties of the Left.

What of the former Communist countries, the neo-Bonapartist states that are now shuffling their way toward "free market" capitalism and that still provide investment opportunity? The more capitalist they are, the more precarious is the general condition of the majority of their populations, while as always an upper stratum of bureaucrats, managers of state enterprises, and agents of international capital lives increasingly well. "Vietnam's leaders [yesterday's Communists] clearly believe that despite the initial 'pain,' the free market will eventually modernize their country. In fact, the restructuring that has been carried out is destroying nearly all the social benefits—job and social security, education, health care, basic public sanitation, even food availability—needed to maintain a vibrant, prosperous society."[11] In China, under more stringent state control, living conditions were improving significantly until quite recently. In the present phase, which is based much more on foreign investment and increasing sell-offs of state enterprises, inequality and unemployment have risen, and the very investments that were expected to be engines of progress now threaten to burden China with overcapacity, and even more unemployment. As in classical Third World countries, these economic problems are accompanied by political repression, which U.S. multinational corporations doing

214    THE STATE IN MODERN SOCIETY

business with China try desperately to downplay. The Cuban case is not relevant to this discussion because of the intervening variable of the blockade. It is true, however, that with increasing foreign investment, especially in tourism, corruption, crime, and prostitution there are on the rise.

It is in Eastern Europe, especially Russia, that the consequences of privatization are most apparent. The broad outlines are fairly well known and do not require further review here. State enterprises are being sold off or privatized in the hands of their former managers, who have become wealthy. Business is closely interlocked with organized crime. Unemployment and emiseration are growing. While some workers in the West worry about how little they are paid, many workers in the former Soviet Union often do not get paid at all. The "healthcare" system that was available to all under Communism, even though barely adequate, is in shambles today, and people simply refuse to go to hospitals. Alcoholism is becoming even more of a national disaster than under Stalin or during the times of the czars.

In the former Yugoslavia, with the exception of Slovenia, the economies are in ruins due to the dislocations of on-again off-again civil wars and population displacements. Poland has become a German neocolony, providing cheap labor for the branch plants and subcontractors of multinational firms, quasi-legal labor in vast German construction projects (while German construction workers are unemployed), and domestics for the homes of wealthy and even not-so-wealthy Germans. Ethnic strife is rampant, anti-Semitism even without Jews is widespread, racist and neo-Nazi skinhead violence has become a daily occurrence, and Roma people ("gypsies") are physically endangered on a daily basis.

In the European post-Soviet world, the Czech Republic and Poland are among the very few nations that have relatively stable parliamentary states. Almost all the rest are ruled by nationalist autocrats with neo-fascist leanings. This should not be surprising, since no class forces strong enough to create a different kind of state exist. There is still resistance to such autocrats (sometimes only on the Internet!), despite their criminal connections and access to weaponry. But it will likely be a considerable time before the internal contradictions of these chaotic states (mainly, the one between the necessity of feeding and housing the population, and the counterproductive racketeering of the "leaders," with the consequent negative impact on economic rebuilding and even ordinary capitalist investment) will trigger the massive eruptions needed to tear these societies away from their neo-Bonapartist regimes. Some oppositional class forces will first have to congeal, and it is hard to predict now what these forces will look like. Nevertheless, gangster oligarchies have fallen before (Nicaragua under the Somozas, Greece under the colonels, etc.), and they will again.

The struggle to hold the line on social benefits, and even to restore those that have been lost, is strongest in western and southern Europe, where working-class parties and labor unions have long histories. It has proven possible, even in recent years, to wring concessions from the state and from capital. The clearest example of this was France in 1968, when many thought a revolution was imminent. But a set of concessions, mediated by the Communist Party and its unions, defused the crisis. President DeGaulle was clearly prepared to declare martial law and turn the country into a dictatorship if these concessions had not worked. That is the dilemma: the power of capital and the states that in varying degree obey it is such that movements can extort reforms up to a point so long as capital thinks it can afford them. At the point that reforms prove to be insufficient, or when capitalist states conclude that the economy cannot afford further reforms, repression remains as an option.

When will reforms become insufficient? When will capitalist states weaken so as to open the road to revolutionary transformations? Reforms become insufficient when subordinate classes become politically more conscious and more organized. That is when capital also becomes weakened and divided and the road to social change opens. The reverse is true as well: as crisis intensifies and impacts not only the victims, but the perpetrators, the ruling class is likely to become divided as to strategy, opening up new possibilities for social change. The process feeds on itself. But, as we have painfully learned from the German experience, that is also the time when movements of antimodernity, nationalism, xenophobia, and old-fashioned fascism, the forces of unreason, also grow. A specter still haunts Europe, and now the entire world, the specter not of communism in the 1848 sense, but certainly of revolution, however defined. But for the victims of capitalism in crisis, there is another specter, that of 1933. It is a ghost that can only be exorcised by internationally oriented, anticapitalist, democratic movements to defend democratic rights and propose positive reforms, even the kind of fundamental reforms that can reconstruct society.

No state in modern society has represented the working class and its allies among other strata except very briefly (the Paris Commune, the early years of the Soviet Union, parts of Spain during the civil war). Every effort to establish a workers' state, with new structures appropriate to the rule of that class, has been defeated either directly by counterrevolutionary forces, or indirectly by creeping bureaucratization and the development of the bureaucracy as a new ruling class. Or it has been co-opted by minimal reforms of the New Deal or even the Swedish variety. Is it completely utopian even to pose the idea of a new form of state, based on the present subordinate classes, as an alternative? Is capitalism the end of history?

It is conceivable that capitalism will survive until the earth has been completely stripped of its natural resources in order to feed the Leviathan of profit. Or it may be that the population will die off due to nuclear war, accident, pollution, starvation, environmental disasters, or diseases that lay waste to civilization because intelligent planning and humane healthcare systems are inconsistent with profit. It is conceivable that greed will triumph. But it is not inevitable.

So in the end we can choose: states such as those described in this volume that operate on behalf of exploiting minorities, as in the past and in the present, or states that truly represent, through genuinely democratic political structures, today's subordinate classes, the majority of the population. Which will it be: Leviathan, or Utopia?

## NOTES

1. The quotation is condensed from the 1985 Jewish Publication Society edition of the *Tanakh*. *Leviathan* is the title of Thomas Hobbes's (1588–1679) famous work, published in 1651 (reprint, New York: Liberal Arts Press, 1948).

2. Robert J. S. Ross and Kent C. Trachte, *Global Capitalism: The New Leviathan* (Albany, N.Y.: State University of New York Press, 1990), 224.

3. Edward S. Herman, "The Global Attack On Democracy, Labor, and Public Values," *Dollars and Sense*, no. 213 (September–October 1997): 12. See also idem, "Privatization: Downsizing Government For Principle and Profit," *Dollars and Sense*, no. 210 (March–April 1997).

4. Richard DuBoff, "Globalization and Wages: The Down Escalator," *Dollars and Sense*, no. 213 (September–October 1997), 40.

5. Saskia Sassen, *Losing Control? Sovereignty in an Age of Globalization* (New York: Columbia University Press, 1996), 28.

6. Ellen Meiskins Wood, "Labor, the State, and Class Struggle," *Monthly Review* 49, no. 2 (July–August 1997): 12.

7. Kathleen J. Tierney, "Toward a Critical Sociology of Risk," *Sociological Forum* 14, no. 2 (1999), 235.

8. Doug Henwood, "Does Globalization Matter?" *In These Times* (March 31, 1997).

9. Daniel Singer, "Requiem for Social Democracy?" *Monthly Review* 48, no. 8 (January 1997): 10.

10. Ibid., 11.

11. Nhu T. Le, "Screaming Souls," review of *Vietnam: Anatomy of a Peace*, by Gabriel Kolko, *Nation* (November 3, 1997).

# INDEX

Abraham, David, 136, 138, 140
Adorno, T. W., 125–26
African National Congress, 34
Agency for International Development, U.S. (AID), 43
Albania, 151
Algeria, 180
Allende, Salvador (president of Chile), 40, 42
Amnesty International, 39–41, 49
anti-Semitism, 187, 198, 214
Arbenz, Jacobo (president of Guatemala), 190
Arendt, Hannah, 123, 140–41, 147, 150
Argentina, 36, 49
Aristide, Jean-Bertrand (president of Haiti), 47
Armenians, 188
Austria, 19, 20, 147, 179, 183
automobile industry, 107–108, 204

autonomy. *See* state, autonomy of

B-2 bomber, 101–102
Baluchistan, 48
Bangkok, Thailand, 45
Berlin Wall, 147
Bhutto, Zulfikar Ali, 38, 39, 48
Bismarck, 20
Black Panther party, 195
Blum, Leon, 21
Bolivar, Simon, 34–35
Bolivia, 44
Bosnia, 168
bourgeoisie, 47–48, 148–49
Brazil, 43, 48–51, 171, 212
Bulgaria, 180
Bush, George, 109

Canada, 74
capitalism, 18, 22, 33, 57–58, 69, 95, 171, 197, 206, 212–13, 216